Wakefield Press

MUG SHOTS

Also by Barry Oakley

Fiction

A Wild Ass of a Man

A Salute to the Great McCarthy

Let's Hear it for Prendergast

Walking Through Tigerland

The Craziplane

Don't Leave Me

Non-fiction

Scribbling in the Dark

Minitudes: Diaries 1974–1997

Plays

The Feet of Daniel Mannix

Beware of Imitations

Bedfellows

A Lesson in English

Marsupials and Politics: Two Comedies

The Ship's Whistle

Scanlan

Music

MUG SHOTS

a memoir

BARRY OAKLEY

Wakefield Press
1 The Parade West
Kent Town
South Australia 5067
www.wakefieldpress.com.au

First published 2012
Reprinted 2013

In a passage about the decline of the *Times On Sunday* newspaper in the first printing of *Mug Shots*, it is stated that the then editor Robert Haupt sacked Valerie Lawson. This was not the case, and the author apologises for the error.

Edited by Julia Beaven, Wakefield Press
Cover designed by Liz Nicholson, designBITE
Designed and typeset by Clinton Ellicott, Wakefield Press
Printed in Australia by Griffin Digital, Adelaide

National Library of Australia Cataloguing-in-Publication entry

Author:	Oakley, Barry, 1931– .
Title:	Mug shots: a memoir / Barry Oakley.
ISBN:	978 1 74305 167 2 (pbk.).
Subjects:	Oakley, Barry, 1931– .
	Authors, Australian – Biography.
Dewey Number:	A823.3

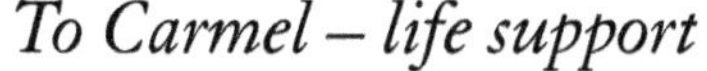

To Carmel – life support

How dost, fool?
Dost dialogue with thy shadow?

Timon of Athens

Teeth

My mouth is wide open and my brother Gavan is peering into it. It is 1970. He's not long back from America and keen to try his new expertise on me. He wears a pale-blue gown and mad-scientist magnifying glasses as he picks and prods. Newly Mastered in Dental Science, he is the Isambard Kingdom Brunel of bridges, and he's going to construct a tricky one across the gap between my lower teeth. It's called a Maryland Bridge, the first to be built in this country.

Lifting his mask so I won't miss a word, he explains that despite innumerable injections there may well be some pain: a payback, he jokes, for what I did to him when we were kids. Like the Chinese burns inflicted on him when he sat on my school lunch. Or my pushing him into deep water off St Kilda pier.

With a mouthful of cotton logs, all I could do was shake my head. 'Intra osseus,' he seemed to say to the nurse. Os? Latin for bone? Into the bone? He moved in on me with the kind of syringe vets use on large animals. Shouldn't it be osseum, the accusative? Had he forgotten how I helped him with Latin grammar?

He sank the nightmare instrument deep into the gum, then the bone, beyond the reach of novocaine. I yelped, and prayed for numbness. Then he began his drilling, with a device that could have broken concrete. I yelped again. Oblivious, he stepped back, admired his excavations and began photographing each step.

'This is the tricky bit. If the cement sets too soon, you'll have metal half in and half out of your mouth, and I'll be halfway down the street.' But it worked, and the furled lips, pitted teeth and bleeding gums would one day be studied by dental pornographers, and my food properly masticated at last.

At one stage, as he moved in close, I noticed a small white scar on top of his right ear. It was the mark left when a truck backed over him in 1938 when he was playing in the gutter outside our house. A back wheel had missed his head by a fraction of an inch. He was carried inside bleeding and screaming, but according to the rapidly summoned Dr Darcy, otherwise unharmed.

It had been Dr Darcy – horn-rimmed, pin-striped and reeking of chloroform – who etherised me on our dining-room table and removed my adenoids – mysterious entities somewhere behind the nose. He was a brusque little man who was held, as doctors were then, in inordinate respect. 'Clean up your room – Doctor's coming.'

The Christian Brothers (quickly)

Nineteen thirty-eight was also the year I began at the Christian Brothers' College in St Kilda – when, one February morning, I was dragged screaming down the driveway behind their residence into a seething quadrangle – a brief anarchy before a whistle was blown, order imposed, and I was enclosed in a regimen that would last ten years. It was not a preparation for life but an intensification of it. When, in life, are you publicly strapped? When do forty of your peers see you blush as you suffer the teacher's ridicule?

It was weakness that was despised, by both teachers and kids. If you were strapped and cried (I managed never to), if you fainted (as I once did during a graphic description of a compound fracture – 'Take that boy out, will you?') or worst of all vomited (as Kevin Cherry did across two desks – to be ostracised at lunchtime from then on) your humiliation was absolute. School was the kind of test that belonged at the end of life, not the beginning.

With brother Gavan at the Estate Agents' picnic, 1939.

War broke out when I was in third class, and the Christian Brothers' College had its similarities: you too had been conscripted, uniformed and sergeant-majored. And in third class you moved up to the front line. If you didn't get the sums Brother Egan wrote up on the blackboard right you were strapped. Sometimes, when most didn't make it, we'd line up on the platform in pairs. Your and your classmate's hands were held out together, so one strap did the work of two: mathematics in action.

In my first year of secondary school I sat next to Eric Donnelly. Eric was dexterous, and devised an ingenious rubber-band-and-ruler mechanism which, when the lid of the desk was closed, would make a tongue poke up from a paper face pasted over the inkwell. He became a surgeon and did missionary work in Papua New Guinea. When an operation on a tribesman failed and he died, a nun was axed to death in a classroom as payback. Eric blamed himself, and when he visited me years later in Richmond he was unhinged. The world, he told us, was running out of silver nitrate, which would mean the end of photography. In the meantime, he said, we must look at our walls. 'See?' he said. 'Look hard – Christ's Holy Shroud face is imprinted there – can't you see?' Eric is buried in Africa somewhere, in the loneliest of lonely graves.

This was also the year I became close to Dick Hughes, who occupied a nearby desk. We had the greatest of teachers, a layman called J.P. Ward, a tall raw-boned man in a worn blue suit, who salted his teaching with stories of his early days in country schools: snakes in the classroom, disembowelling by an enraged boar of a man thrown from his horse, bush hermits raving mad from loneliness, goannas big enough to kill a dog.

The stories had an invariable beginning: 'Up bush,

thirty-odd years ago,' which was enough to send Hughes and all those luckless enough to sit near him into implosions of giggles. Mr Ward had a scooter tyre as a strap, and the more his stories set us off, the angrier he'd get. Dick would start his giggling, the whole row would shake, and a cabal would be summoned out the front to put out our hands for, as Mr Ward termed it, 'a smack'.

Hughes was also a master mimic. He'd developed a passion for Dixieland jazz, and his specialty was an imitation of the great drummer Gene Krupa 'in a frenzy'. He'd wait for a Brother to turn to the blackboard, and while the voyages of Magellan were being sketched out, Hughes would do his imitations with two whirring rulers, soundlessly, stopping the moment the Brother turned to face us. His neighbours would laugh but the phantom drummer would not: strappings again.

I had only one skill, and that was tennis. I still have a photo of the 1944 school team, my bone-thin arms cradling one of those racquets with flattened tops that went back to the days of Henry VIII. You went out on the orange gravel en-tout-cas (the word has disappeared) and because you represented your school, your racquet became heavy, your strokes uncertain and often you lost. Top sport is about temperament. Neurotics didn't have a hope.

Operatic Melbourne

After Pearl Harbour and the Japanese drive south, trenches were dug in the parks, air raid shelters in the backyards, and Air Raid Wardens appointed to ensure windows were blacked out at night. Wooden shutters shielded the light of the trams, with their drivers' compartments in total darkness – you could hear but not see them. At night, Melbourne was a dark and scary place, a set for an opera that was never produced.

The Oakley family had moved from number eleven Montague Avenue to number four, directly opposite. But there was a grand finale beforehand. Number eleven had flaunted above its front gate a large banner on which was painted GRAND BAZAAR. FOOD FOR BRITAIN FUND. STALLS, LUCKY DIPS, RAFFLES. In an unprecedented display of communal feeling, neighbours had gathered in our lounge to organise it, chaired by the masterful Mr Reginald Green who'd been spared military service because he was in charge of much of Melbourne's electricity supply.

The highlight was Mr Green's creation in our garage (empty, because our father was away at the war). Spotlit at its end were portraits of Musso, Adolf and Tojo, all with the twisted evil look that Armstrong captured in his *Argus* cartoons. Get a tennis ball through one of their gaping maws and you won a prize. Overall, we raised an unprecedented thirty-three pounds ten shillings.

The Japanese might have been getting closer, but we'd already been invaded. American soldiers were everywhere. They crowded St Kilda's Esplanade, looking for diversions in this end-of-the-world city. They were polite, their uniforms were tailored (a painful contrast to the Australians' hessian bagginess), their staff cars were late-model Buicks, and if you rode your bike down to Fisherman's Bend and parked it by the airstrip fence, you could watch Kittyhawks, Lightnings and Bostons roar in a few feet over your head.

A rat-grey Messerschmitt 109 fighter was exhibited at

Melbourne Town Hall, and you were allowed to climb into its cockpit – it was metallic and claustrophobic, and seemed to smell of Nazi Germany. Later in the war, a Japanese midget submarine also did a tour, and one could crawl into a confinement even more totalitarian. For a schoolboy, wartime Melbourne was pure excitement.

Ours and theirs

Perhaps the Axis Powers didn't worry us because we were living in a benign totalitarianism of our own, ruled by a dictator of our own – Archbishop Daniel Mannix. It was Mannix who Confirmed a church-full of schoolboys, followed it up with an interminable homily, and then tried to persuade us to pledge to abstain from one of the few permitted Catholic pleasures – alcohol – until we were twenty-one. 'Stand up those boys manly enough to do it,' he said. Many stood, the intrepid did not, and I, in a posture that would perhaps prove typical, half-rose in a crouch.

Below Mannix in the authoritarian pyramid was the parish priest, and below that CBC St Kilda's headmaster, the urbane Brother Rooney, MA (a rare distinction then). One day early in 1945 Rooney told the assembly that people might be wondering what a big school like ours was doing for the war effort. He had the answer: a cadet unit.

Rooney had already filled me with dread with two earlier announcements: dancing and debating were arts we needed to learn. We trained for the first with our classmates as partners on the school handball court. ('Boys,' said the mustachioed instructor, 'once you learn you'll go dancing eight nights a week.') This was followed by anthropological ordeals with the girls from Presentation Convent, closely supervised – 'You, go and dance with that fat girl over there.' I never mastered the complex art of conversing, doing the Pride of Erin and concealing signs of sexual excitement all at the same time.

Debating was even more frightening. My maiden effort, in 1944, lives with me still. I went out the front with my little speech on helicopters ready, but couldn't raise my eyes to the class. Staring at the floor I declared, in a quavering voice, that they were now 'a practical proposition'. I was right, but my delivery was without conviction, and the case was lost.

I failed to dance or debate, and now there were richer possibilities for failure: cadets. It was voluntary, but everyone had to join, and soon all the Leaving Certificate class – small boys and big boys, skinny boys and wide boys – were bagged in khaki sacking.

We were used to taking orders, but not from our classmates. The ambitious went off to do courses, and came back as cadet lieutenants in smart uniforms with Sam Browne belts across their chests and pips on the shoulders. The go-getters and the no-getters were now clearly defined, and every Friday afternoon the first were put in charge of the second.

We would assemble before portly Brother Lewis ('Thunderbum') corseted in captain's uniform. He'd bark out orders ('Hand away from your face, McCarthy!') then each platoon would stride into the adjoining Alma Park, where we were taught to slope and present arms, and sent on mindless marches round the oval.

This would build up to something even worse – cadet camp. What was the point if, a week before, Japan had surrendered?

Never mind, we had a double holiday. We celebrated the Feast of the Assumption of the Blessed Virgin Mary on 15 August, and on 16 August there was V-J Day. Victory was scrawled everywhere, blackboards included. 'People trickled into churches to give thanks,' admonished one newspaper, 'but there was the usual sprinkling of exhibitionists who thrive on mass revelry and wallow in the licence of unrestrained behaviour . . . to sing Tipperary in an absurdly high key, to dance jitterbug-style in a cramped space, and play two-up in a laneway.'

A week later, the war over and everyone going home, we were under canvas at Watsonia Army Camp, maybe in training for the next one. The first night we returned to our straw-stuffed palliasses stunned. We'd just seen a hygiene film crude even by schoolboy standards. It showed a soldier with diarrhoea on a latrine, wiping himself clumsily afterwards, not washing his hands, then getting into a bread delivery van, where he sits on the loaves and has a smoke.

It was the beginning of a process of brutalisation that would last a week, and it started to come out in our language. There was no sentence in which fuck could not be used, as verb, noun, adjective or participle. One morning, at the rifle range, we were told not to touch the triggers of our 303s before receiving the command to fire. 'These bullets are live fuckers,' warned the sergeant, showing a creative use of the word. Somehow, Dick Hughes's rifle went off. 'What fucking fuckwit did that?' he shouted. The applications of the word seemed endless.

Sleep was difficult, discipline unrelenting, the food inedible. (Cook, ladling out treacly-brown curry into our pannikins: 'This'll make you shit.' It did, but to the horror of middle-class sensitives like myself, the lavatory bowls were uncubicled. The shy had to take to the bushes or hang on and go in the dark.)

I celebrated my return to civilian life by going to the Palais to see Abbott and Costello in *Lost in a Harem*. How pleasant to escape to the Arabian kingdom of Barabeeha, ruled by the wicked sultan Nimativ ('Take him to the dungeon! The damp one!'). And the beautiful Marilyn Maxwell, and Jimmy Dorsey's band marching through the bazaar in turbans. Apart from Churchill, Eisenhower and Curtin, no one did more for the war effort than Abbott and Costello. They made us laugh when that was what the world needed most.

The Christian Brothers defended

How to explain a regimen predicated on a God of love and mercy, where the Hail Mary was said every hour and the strap used in between? Where sanctity and savagery co-existed? The Brothers would have called it discipline, of the kind needed for the formation of the Christian gentleman. This fabled boy was neatly dressed in school uniform, his cap straight and his socks pulled up. He treated others with respect – especially girls, with whom he'd never contemplate going further than a passionless kiss on the cheek.

The Brothers were like disadvantaged parents, determined that their boys were going to do better – as doctors, lawyers, public servants, or, best of all, priests. They were hard on us because their lives depended on it. If we proved intractable to their shaping, their vocation meant nothing. They trained us like athletes, to win.

The notion of sacrifice in the Christian Brothers ideal is now virtually incomprehensible. I can still recall the cheap boarding-house smell of cabbage that hung around the back stairs of their residence. There was none of the glamour of priestliness in their calling. It was a life of plain food and plain rooms and weekend loneliness. No wife, no family, just the constant classroom grind: calculus, Bunsen burners, beam balances, isosceles triangles, the latent heat of fusion – all set within the demanding frame of Christian doctrine.

It was as relentless for them as it was for us, but because we were force-fed with the learning and literature of the Western world, we were, paradoxically, set free. The fact that a couple of them broke under the pressure and preyed on the students they were supposed to be educating makes what the majority managed to achieve all the more impressive.

Languor and longing

When the tea had been consumed, Oblomov raised himself upon his elbow and came within an ace of getting out of bed. Glancing at his slippers, he even began to extend a foot in that direction, but then withdrew it.

At the beginning of 1948, convinced by the four honours I'd gained in the matriculation examination that I was destined for higher things, I resembled Goncharov's fictional Russian aristocrat, who spent the first 150 pages of the novel in bed.

Freed from the disciplines of school and study, I aestivated (*OED*: 'to spend the summer in a state of stupor'). I was too old for Luna Park and St Kilda Beach, but not old enough for anything else.

Girls filled me with terror. I peeped through the gaps in the paling fence at Heather, who pranced about in tight tops and shorts. Worse – her bathroom was above our bedroom window, and the sound of her singing as she showered, her bosomy pinkness diffused by the frosted glass, tormented me nightly.

The phrase 'late developer' could have been invented for me. I still haven't forgotten my shock when Dick Hughes explained to me how the sexual act was performed. We were both fourteen. Hughes had just learned the facts from his foreign correspondent father Richard, and arranged a meeting immediately. The conversation went something like this.

He: 'The male does go into the female. We were right.'

Me: 'From the rear, like dogs do it?'

He: 'From the front.'

Me: 'Face to face? Staring at one another? Are you sure?'

He: 'I'm sure.'

Me: 'Think of the embarrassment. It'd have to be done in the dark . . . so that's what fucking means.'

He: 'No. It means preparing to go to bed.'

Me: 'And rape?'

He (authoritatively): 'Clutching the private parts.'

I had then gone to the dusty medical books in our oak bookcase. (It was thought my father had once studied medicine, a myth he made no effort to dispel.) I saw in one of them clinical drawings of bodily organs, including the pudenda (gerundive form of pudere, to be ashamed). I was now trapped between two irreconcilable polarities. On the one hand the Pride of Erin and the Circular Waltz, and on the other the indecent internality of the dance's ultimate end.

My Oblomovian condition was aggravated by what happened on one of the rare mornings I ventured up to the shops to do the messages (as they used to be called) for my mother. I was struck, as if by a dart, with the sight of Valerie G. Valerie lived round the corner from us, and in her school uniform had attracted only moderate attention. But this was the summer holidays, and she was now sixteen and had turned into something else. Was calyx right? Was that the word I'd learned at school for the leaves around a flower when in bud? Valerie's uniform was a calyx, and out of it this striking creature had blossomed. I followed her in her golden summer garment at a due distance, like a dog. In days, dizziness had turned to love.

At this time I'd also become infatuated with literature. In matriculation, the saintly Brother Kilmartin, the best teaching Brother I'd ever had, had paid me a compliment that turned me crimson. 'Mr Moloney,' he'd said at the end of the final term, 'has topped the class in English . . . Mr Oakley's success may come later.'

Still unemployed, I bought a Penguin – *A History of English Literature* by B. Ifor Evans – from which, seated at a card table on our front verandah, I took notes. A topography emerged, a landscape. The further I penetrated into the book, the more altitude I gained. By the end, I felt like an alpinist looking over an entire territory, from Beowulf to T.S. Eliot.

Conflate late-adolescent romantic suspiration with literary aspiration and the result (I quote from a diary of the time) is beyond satire: *I walked the warm streets with hopeful eyes – in vain, in vain*. In recording occasional sightings, I succeeded in being embarrassing in two languages: *Oui! Mutual regards. Je pouvais penser à rien d'autre*. Fantasies flower: *Put on père's dressing gown and stood before the mirror, as if after a dramatic plane crash, with V watching.*

The temporary trustees

By April my father, lubricated after one of his nightly visits to the South Yarra Club (to be punished with a dried-up dinner) announced it was time I got a job. He still had a faint hope I could be groomed to take over his business – A.E. Oakley, Real Estate Agents – and secured for me what he called a position with the Perpetual Trustee Company.

A 'position'? I learned on my first day, when I pushed open the hissing glass doors and inhaled the catacomb odours of deceased estates, that this meant 'office boy'. I was briskly welcomed by Miss Durant, a tall cassowary of a woman who ruled the front office. These were the days of desk blotters and inkwells, and it was going to be my job to fill them every morning. She produced large bottles of blue and red ink, with which I was to begin with the Managing Director's office, continue along the ground floor (Trusts) then work my way up to Accounts and Property.

The Managing Director, impressively named W. Earle Orr, was too important to arrive early. His sanctuary was large and his desk presidential, though almost totally bare: two telephones, a leather-bound diary, and brass desk set with an imperial pair of pens. I tiptoed in, sniffing a stale-cigar bouquet of important business, performed my task, and tiptoed out.

When I returned later, three floors of inkwells filled, Miss Durant pranced towards me, holding up a typed letter. 'What is this?'

'It's a letter, Miss Durant.'

'A most important letter. Do you notice the signature?' W. Earle Orr had signed it, in bronze ink. I'd put red ink in his blue inkwell, and vice versa. W. Earle Orr now appeared in his

Dreading the prospect of a career with the Perpetual Trustees, 1948.

doorway, horn-rimmed and expensively suited. He was holding up a second letter, similarly signed. He shook his head, made a managerial roaring sound, then stormed back into his office.

Inexplicably, I was soon promoted to Front Counter, and a few weeks later became an Assistant Trusts Officer, and given a small desk behind the office of Mr Simmons, whom I was supposed to be Assisting. Simmons, who sported a fighter-pilot's moustache (he'd been one) would push back a glazed window, hand me a will, and ask me to work out the tax payable on the estate.

It didn't take long for him to realise he'd been saddled with a gawky seventeen-year-old incapable of understanding the principles of commerce. 'You're not cut out for this,' he gritted through his little open window, and he was right. But neither was he. How could a man who had driven (his word) Spitfires adjust to a commercial necropolis, where correspondence ('In reply to yours of the third ultimo . . .') was copied in two colours, green for the running files and pink for the records, and stored in rows in the basement?

In the space between will and codicil, there'd be flick-the-cardboard – a diversion devised by two other ATOs who worked further along what they revelled in calling 'the back passage'. One would frisbee the cardboard to the other, and then to me, and back again, sometimes going dangerously close to the top of the partition that separated the Trust Officers from us. One afternoon Tim Reidy, after a counter lunch, flicked too hard. The cardboard curved over the partition and caught Mr Appleby, deep in discussion with a client, across the cheek. Reidy was demoted to office boy.

Since I'd now shown incompetence in two fields, when I was summoned to the Assistant Manager's office I hoped for the best – that I'd be fired. The aptly named Mr Wood, bald, bespectacled and bloodless, invited me to take a seat. The company had plans for me to do a university commerce course in the evenings at their expense. This was worse than the sack. 'Well,' he said, puzzled at my lack of response, 'what do you say?' I leaned back in my chair, trying to look flattered, lost my balance and did a backwards somersault onto the carpet. I didn't have to say anything. He looked down at me, and I looked up at him. I wasn't for business, and business wasn't for me.

There'd only been one excitement in my six months at the Perpetual Trustees, and that was the trip in. By the time the roaring, bull-nosed Reo reached the Alma Road stop, it was packed. The foolhardy would make a leap at the bottom step, gain a foothold, and ride riskily into the city. My companion in foolhardiness was a young man called Edwin Shirley, who managed to do all of the above and light a cigarette at the same time.

Edwin was slow of thought and attenuated of body, but I had reason to cultivate him as we rode dangerously together on the bottom step of the bus. He lived in a rambling old house opposite Valerie's. So when he invited me to call on him one Saturday afternoon, I accepted. With his fat dog Bingo waddling behind us, he showed me over the place, leading me eventually to his parents' bedroom. Around three sides, piled along the floor, were rows of empty whisky bottles. Mr and Mrs Shirley, who used to dress in their best every Saturday afternoon and go to one of Melbourne's best hotels, were alcoholics.

Speak to her, now!

And their strange son, I was about to learn, was a pyromaniac. 'Come on out,' said Edwin, smiling in anticipation. I followed him and the barrelled Bingo to the front verandah, where there was a large stand of bamboo. He crouched down and flicked his cigarette lighter until he got a blaze started, and as it leaped up and spread he looked at me, then back at it, rapt. 'The hose!' I shouted. 'Get the hose!' But Edwin was a pyro connoisseur – he waited, then moved calmly to the hose, quelling the blaze just before the verandah went up. Would Valerie have noticed? Valerie had not.

But there were possibilities here, and my diary entry of the time is too bad not to quote: *In the midst of a purple summer twilight, my brother says there's a fire at Edwin's place. A thousand hopes spill my mind over. We hurry up; glow of golden fire in the overgrown garden. And the spectators!*

Valerie was one of them, in a tight white sweater, with her silly little dog. And we were there, with our silly little dog. I worked my way into the crowd now forming as the fire moved into the overgrown thicket. It was creeping towards the house, where Edwin was exultantly waiting with the hose, and I was creeping towards Valerie, who now spoke, not to but at me, not really noticing.

'The house'll go up.'

'No, it wont,' I said, 'he'll save it at the last minute. You watch.' She watched, we watched – together, watching! – as Edwin moved in on the blaze, doused it, then raised his hands over his head like a prizefighter.

The crowd was dispersing. Speak to her, quickly! I was saved by our dogs. In oblivious canine echoes of my fantasies, her little dog was having its hindquarters investigated by ours, only to have its advances snappily rejected. We had a little communal laugh in the dusk, and that was it, except for my diary. As my spirits went up, the prose continued downwards: *Oh joy! Unhurried ecstasy, words, and looks in the dim light.*

Prone at last

Since I seemed suited to nothing else, teaching was all that was left. You gained entry to the profession by beginning as a student teacher. After an interview, a menacing memorandum arrived in the mail from one E.H. Wheeler, Secretary, Education Department. He wished to inform me that I had been appointed as a student teacher ON PROBATION at School No. 1896, Hornby Street, Windsor, subject to the conditions set out hereunder . . . 'Should you not comply with these conditions, steps will be taken to dispense with your services, unless you can submit satisfactory reasons for your failure to do so . . . On taking up this appointment, you may claim a refund of the fare paid for travelling from your home address to the school, provided the cost is 5 shillings or over. Trains, trams or other established services must be used wherever practicable. Preference, however, should be given to trains.'

Hornby Street State School was a dismal Victorian pile down a side street in what was then the working-class suburb of Windsor. A student teacher, I soon learned, was neither. One stood on the platform facing the class and feeling foolish, while the teachers taught. The kids knew you were a nobody, and treated you accordingly, and the teachers often had you run errands. I was an office boy again.

There were two other student teachers, both girls. In my deprived state I was attracted to both of them, but crippled as I was by shyness it was up to them to make a move, and one of them, Jane, eventually did. Her parents, she told me, were away Saturday afternoons. Was this an invitation, or just general information?

'Would it be . . . would it be possible . . . okay . . .?' I bumbled.

'Oh, for God's sake,' said Jane, 'come over.'

The next Saturday afternoon I told my mother I was going to see Dick Hughes. Tingling with erotic terror, I walked down Inkerman Road, turned a corner, paused at the gate of a dauntingly large house, and knocked. Jane welcomed me in a translucent muslin shift that failed to conceal the outline of her bra.

Jane was already an experienced drinker, and I was not. She parted the panels of a large cabinet, revealing an arsenal of bottles, their reflections vulgarly mirrored.

'Pimm's? G&T?'

'Pardon?'

'Gin and tonic.'

'Yes, please.' I'd never smelt gin before, let alone tasted it, and the combination unseated me. I offered her a Craven A to show I could be sophisticated too. 'Try one of these,' she said, opening a box whose contents glowed brown and gold. I'd only just mastered the drawback, and inhaled an exotic Sobranie in the Humphrey Bogart manner. The room seemed to tremble slightly. I sipped at my G&T. The room now began a slow revolve, like a restaurant. Jane blew a perfect smoke ring. The couch too was moving, and I needed to lie on it. What began as a saunter ended with a rugby tackle. Prone at last!

'You okay?'

'Dizzy spell. Sorry.'

'It's the Sobranie – they're strong.'

Jane sat on the couch beside me. Through half-closed eyes she had a vague resemblance to Rita Hayworth. She was smirking. Her girlfriends were going to hear about this.

'Am I going round in circles, or is it the room?'

'It's you, kid, it's you.'

'You'd better stop me then.'

I put my hand on her freckled forearm and drew her, in the language of Millsing and Booning, towards me.

I was eighteen, and never been kissed. Eighteen, and never

unzipped a dress. ('It's at the back, darling.') I stared at her lacy Berlei, and then she turned away. Had I gone too far?

'Undo them. Can you do that?'

'Of course.' My hands were shaking, and the hooks were tiny. 'Sorry. I'm a naif.'

'You're a what?'

'Naif – the noun from naive, the adjective.'

'You're good with words, I'll give you that.'

'It's the only thing I'm good at.'

'Wrap your nouns round these then.'

Jane undid herself expertly, releasing breasts enhanced by a few freckles. I gaped. I was speechless.

From then on I paid Jane regular visits. ('You *are* close to Dick Hughes,' said my mother.) I tried Pimm's No. 1 Cup, rum and Coke, even crème de menthe, but never got further than having my way with her breasts. The richer fonts lower down (Rape of Lucrece) were out of bounds in 1949, and I was perfectly happy with what I got.

The code we had at the time, grading sexual success from one to ten, should not be taken amiss by feminists – it suggested girls' sheer unattainability. One, I think, meant no more than actually talking to the girl of one's desire, two the breakthrough of holding hands, three a kiss on the lips, four touching the covered breast, five the same exposed, and so on to the unimaginable heights of ten. When I confided my five to my alibi, Dick Hughes, he was impressed.

Whatever happened to Sloyd?

Despite my Saturday excitements, the weekdays were getting worse. By now I'd been assigned to fifth and sixth grades, where the kids were unbluffable. I'd stand on the platform staring at them, and they'd stare right back at me.

I had to witness occasional strappings, and the tendency of Mr Virtue, the diminutive headmaster, to lean across pubescent girls on the pretext of checking their work. When the teacher of either grade left the room, anarchy prevailed. I spent much of 1949 praying – that I'd not be left on my own in class, that the school might burn down, that I'd contract a painless long-term illness. I sometimes included requests that I'd have the courage to follow up with Valerie, my true love – or, if not, Heather, the girl next door would do. ('Christ almighty,' I imagined God the Father muttering to his Son, 'isn't Jane enough?')

The extra-mural activities were just as bad. As part of our preparation for the trained Primary Teachers' Certificate, there were Theory of Teaching ('Write full notes of a first lesson to Grade IV on The Pronoun'), Penmanship ('Write the following in a free running hand: "He did not see the starlight on the Laspur hills, Nor the far Afghan snow."'), Music (based on the principles of Tonic Sol-fa) and Sloyd.

Sloyd, defined by the *OED* as 'A system of instruction in elementary woodwork originally developed in Sweden', was taught by a dust-coated cockney called Mr Monger, and the ineptitude first shown in my inability to do up shoelaces even in grade three was on display every fortnight. While others progressed to mulga ashtrays, I spent most of the course with cardboard desk blotters.

In the last weeks of this year of humiliations, the portly

figure of R.G. Menzies leaned from his political parapet and saved me, and many others, by introducing Commonwealth Government Scholarships. As my matriculation results had been good, all that stood between me and remote, unknowable university was an interview.

In a suit now two sizes too small for me, with sleeves failing to cover my wrists, I faced an unnerving trio of interrogators. What was my attitude to teaching? Couldn't get enough of it. What did I hope to gain from an Arts degree? More and better teaching. And in the wider, extra-curricular world? It would give shape to my life and thereby help me to shape students' lives. And so your present life is shapeless? (This from a keen, white-haired lady who by now was scenting hypocrisy.) A word came to me, a wonderful word, a winning ace of a word: 'Somewhat inchoate.' The panel stopped staring at me, and stared at each other. I was in.

Months of Sundays

In the late forties, returned-soldier fathers, enjoying the novelty of car ownership, took their families on Sunday drives. Ours followed three ritual paths. My father preferred the Dandenongs – pristine mountains, as yet uninfested by suburbia. Once past Ringwood you were in Arthur Streeton territory; the towns – Olinda, Belgrave, Emerald – had names like birdsong. Their vowels and consonants were liquid, and carried the primeval smell of fern gullies within them. 'I'm just popping in for a few minutes,' our father would say, leaving his wife and two children waiting in the Hillman Minx outside each rural hotel (bona fide travellers permitted).

Sometimes we'd go to Port Melbourne, park overlooking Station Pier and look down at the ships, perhaps from an atavistic urge to escape the Melbourne Sunday, when places of amusement were closed and the streets deserted – except for Acland Street, behind Luna Park, where Jewish people gathered in lively groups and had coffee and cake, affording a frightening glimpse of what the Methodists called the Continental Sunday. Family life was not something carried on in cafes. Meals were best enjoyed in the privacy of the home.

Option three was a trip to the city along St Kilda Road, then lined with mansions (since replaced by sterile shoeboxes). One continued into Swanston Street, where we'd peer up at the Manchester Unity Building, Melbourne's first skyscraper. 'Fourteen floors,' said my father, as we took in this wonder. Then on to dubiously multicultural Carlton. 'That's the university,' my father would say authoritatively, and we'd look over at this steepled enclave, where no Oakley had ever set foot, until a single word took me there.

Unexplored territory

When the time came in 1950 to leave suburbia (at least during the day) where Victas were turning grass into lawn and Hills hoists lifting white washing skyward, I encountered an unnerving absence. Eleven years of roll calls and regulations were replaced by total indifference. There were lectures and tutorials, but whether you went was your business. No one seemed to care what you wore or what you said.

I joined a shabby aristocracy that flaunted rollneck sweaters, duffle coats and sandals. In the University Caf we stirred the world around in our coffee cups and talked of Kafka. Suburbia had to be shed, and no one did it more spectacularly than Barry Humphries, who could be seen in the library studying like everyone else – only he did it with the back of his chair resting on the floor, his long legs waving in the air like a mantis.

I followed the smart money and skipped lectures, until I realised what I was missing. A.D. Hope, in a suit of blue serge even in summer, mumbling on Dostoevsky – memorably if you sat up close. How could this man, who dressed like an inspector of schools, and spoke as if we were sharing not a lecture but a secret, write poetry of such sensuality as *Imperial Adam*? 'She promised on the turf of paradise/ Delicious pulp of the forbidden fruit;/ Sly as the snake she loosed her sinuous thighs.'

Or Ian Maxwell, a small man with an imperial head, intoning *Paradise Lost* from memory ('He'll weep in a minute,' said the student next to me, who was repeating the subject.) Or A.R. Chisholm, an even smaller man with an even bigger head – a head that French erudition seemed to have enlarged, a head that had nodded and noted when listening to some of the giants of French literature, resulting in the following essay subject appearing on the noticeboard: 'Paul Valery once said to me that the poet is himself unaware of some of the images that may radiate to the reader's mind. Discuss.' Or Vin Buckley, smaller still, and compensating with the gravity of his delivery as he opened up *A Portrait of the Artist as a Young Man* for us, still glowing with the shock of the new.

I was entering not one realm but two. After a chance encounter up at the shops, when I was acknowledged, as a queen might a subject, I forced myself into a public phone booth, inhaled its stuffy metallic smells with some calming deep breathing, and dialled Valerie's number, praying I wouldn't get her terrifying Major-General father. Saved: Valerie answered. My suggestion we see Eisenstein's *Alexander Nevsky* at the New Theatre was met with a pause (puzzlement? incredulity?) and then 'okay'.

Though it sounded like grudging agreement, I pressed on, and on the Saturday night I penetrated the G— living room in an ill-fitting gabardine overcoat, and faced the parents, who seemed to start back slightly, as if I were from another planet (I was).

We bussed it into town – my offhandedness a pretence, hers looking like the real thing. Would Eisenstein bond us? I'd seen *Alexander Nevsky* at the university, and told her it was the greatest film ever made, but when the Teutonic Knights advanced over the ice to Prokofiev's music, she laughed. I was offended, and she was bored. The evening was a failure. 'What?' said Dick Hughes afterwards. 'You didn't even get to two?' I'd escorted Valerie to her front gate, it was a moonlit night, and I hadn't even got to two.

Still, there was always the other realm, which gave itself to me at once. Thanks to my university tutors, the doors of the Great Hall of Literature were opened, and after a few preliminary struggles with syntax, I felt completely at home. Yeats was easy, Hopkins and Eliot more difficult. But once their codes were cracked and their meanings broken into, the effort made the pleasure even greater.

It was wonderful to listen to the poets, but the supreme music came from James Joyce. If the *Portrait* gleamed with newness, what could *Ulysses* possibly be like? I hurried into Cheshire's bookshop one Saturday morning and there it was, not long unbanned, between bare green wartime-economy edition boards. I can still remember taking it home on the red bus. It seemed to give off heat, like new-baked bread.

Unguided by introduction or commentary, I sailed through it in wonderment, missing much but getting the free-flowing gist. The old language had been turned into a new language, the old style smelted with something strange and the old respectability opened above and below. A skylight had appeared over the house of fiction, and underneath the literary drawing room a trapdoor gave on to a cellar where instinct and ribaldry ruled.

Ulysses is probably responsible for more bad prose than any other novel, and a modest portion of it was mine. Stream-of-consciousness short stories were speedily sent off to *Melbourne University Magazine*, and just as speedily sent back. All now lost and forgotten, save for one surviving shard: '*He looked past Luna Park with its writhing switchbacks, past the oriental domes of the baths, to the spire-prick and chimney-poke of Melbourne city.*'

If Joyce was leading a literary revolution, Marxists were attempting the same in university politics. There were rousing lunchtime speeches from Labor Club luminaries like Ian Turner and Ken Gott, warning of the class war to come because of the immiseration of the proletariat – who, in the real world, seemed to be doing quite well.

The novelist Frank Hardy, notorious for his crudely carpentered *Power Without Glory*, was once brought in for extra munition. He put on a fiery performance. 'It's people like you lot,' he shouted up at the students ranged around him, 'who'll be the first to go.' That was his thesis and we had the antithesis – a shower of orange peel and paper aeroplanes. He wouldn't have wanted it any other way.

The Labor Club's noise eventually reached the ears of the Melbourne Establishment, which responded in the person of F.L. Edmunds, MLA for Hawthorn. As recalled by Max Marginson, he described university academics as 'socialists, parlour pinks' – and in a pryotechnical final flourish, 'dingoes crowing from their dunghills'.

Are you engagé?

At the same time, there was a quieter revolution afoot across Tin Pan Alley at Newman College. Inside this Mayan/Byzantine fantasy designed by Walter Burley Griffin, Catholic students were engaging in the unprecedented activity of thinking for themselves. They were trying to join together what the Australian Church had put asunder: 'Catholic' and 'intellectual'.

The Newman Society's Ian Turner and Ken Gott were Vincent Buckley and Bill Ginnane. They were the leaders of what was called the intellectual apostolate, quoting French theologians we'd never heard of, to the effect that we had to complete the work of the secular university by opening it up to the sacred. The clergy had always been the leaders, with the laity sheepishly following. Now there was a double reversal: the world was to be affirmed, not denied, and we were the ones who were going to do it.

There were meetings, Masses and summer camps at Point Lonsdale, where an assortment of sandals, shorts and floral dresses, under a tin roof that pinged with the heat, would listen to talks about the power of the incarnation to transform the world. But there were also earthy dissenters who thought the

Plotting a Catholic takeover of Melbourne University in 1953
(from left: the author, Greg O'Loughlin, Des O'Grady, Brian Buckley).

jargon of being engagé with the milieu pretentious. 'What's all this weltanschauung nonsense?' objected one of them. 'Why can't you just say a way of looking at the world?'

And there were parties in Parkville, opposite the university. One night, when I was being hammered by John Dormer, the eccentric heir to an English beer fortune, I beat a backwards retreat – and there in a corner, scarcely able to sit, let alone talk, was Vin Buckley, the guru himself, comatose with liquor. I was shocked. That night, my university education really began.

Archbishop Mannix was uneasily tolerant of the Newman Society, very much preferring a different apostolate, run by B.A. Santamaria, under the superbly meaningless title of The Movement. The Cold War was warming up, and The Movement was on the move. It organised Industrial Groups (Santamaria had a genius for anodyne titles) to infiltrate the Labor Party, and Dr Evatt, Labor's leader, a man of massive intellect and minuscule political acumen, was being sawn off at the knees. The Groups (to their credit) battled the Communists in the unions, and from Catholic pulpits wildlife imagery flourished. While the Reds were white-anting us from within, the priests would inveigh, the Communist octopus was slithering southwards from China, with tentacles poised to embrace us. We were trapped between the termites and the calamari.

For Catholics, the fifties were not a time of suburban torpor. It was always five minutes to midnight. From anonymous offices in Swanston Street, men with briefcases went out to the parishes. At the West St Kilda branch of the Catholic Young Men's Society, which I'd joined to play cricket and football, we were told that unless we got off our backsides, the yellow hordes would soon be swarming through the streets.

Tired of the aerated theologies of the Newman Society and awkward with girls, a few of us retreated to the Campion Society, whose members were earthier, but just as fond of talk. We would gather on a Saturday night round a table forested with bottles, and smoke, drink and talk, often till dawn. Was The Movement sanctioned by the bishops, and therefore Catholic Action? Or was our affiliation with it a matter of choice, and therefore no more than the action of Catholics? Was Santamaria manipulating Mannix, or was it the other way round? My father had his own theory about the Catholics and the Communists. 'They're all in it together.'

Green in the face

After innumerable beery nights in smoke-filled rooms, eight of us decided on a hitchhike round Tasmania. My fellow Campions included Bill Hannan and Ron Fitzgerald, both to become leading educationalists, Kevin Keating, soon to join the Dominican order, Desmond O'Grady, later a writer and Rome correspondent for a number of newspapers, and the prickly Ron Conway.

Conway, who became a prominent Melbourne psychologist, had an unnerving habit of applying his alleged analytic talent to the rest of us. I and one or two others in the group, he confided as we flew to Tasmania, were heading for a crisis. There was indeed a crisis – when we split into two quartets, how to avoid being in the same one as Ron?

Tasmanians proved extraordinarily generous in those innocent times, and trucks and utilities stopped for us, despite our dishevelment and number. I had only two dramas. In the

Not prisoners on day release – Catholic lads on a hitchhike around Tasmania.

first, after we decided to pair off to get quicker lifts, my companion Bernie Barbour and I were dropped off at night beside a paddock. We got through the fence, dug our hip holes, laid our groundsheets and slipped into our sleeping bags.

When I woke up, at dawn, a trio of bulls was giving us close and unwelcoming inspection. It took a lot of whispering to wake Bernie up, which he did to this: 'Don't move.' We didn't move. The bulls didn't move. 'Stay horizontal,' Bernie offered. We stayed horizontal. The bulls continued to stare at us. They looked hard and mean. The farmer that now happened to drive past would have shared their puzzlement. He would have seen two green sleeping bags, caterpillaring like giant pupae towards the fence.

The second trauma came at the end of the hitchhike, when we boarded the geriatric *Taroona* for the trip back to Melbourne. I've always been a poor sailor, dating back to the days when my father took me on fishing trips in Port Phillip Bay, and I'd spend the time seasick in the bottom of the boat, while he tossed empty beer bottles into the water and pulled flathead out of it.

The *Taroona* bucked across Bass Strait all night, and after leaving my lavatory-sized cabin to throw up in the genuine one, I couldn't find my way back, and opened a succession of identical doors onto a variety of snoring and suffering passengers, before finally finding my own. Much to my embarrassment (twenty-one, and still a mummy's boy) my mother was at Port Melbourne to greet me, and looked shocked: 'You're green in the face.'

Ron, myself and the mystic marriage

After this adventure, Ron Conway had taken a puzzling fancy to me. He would invite me to his Middle Park cottage where he lived with his mother, usher me into a room crammed with books and records – he was the Catholic *Advocate*'s music critic at the time – put on a Mahler symphony, and we'd share its rhapsodic transcendencies in silence. Sometimes, in the middle of an epiphany, there'd be a timid knock on the door. Ron, not pleased, would open it a few inches only. A pallid hand would pass him a plate of biscuits, then the door would be smartly closed. I never saw more of his mother than her fingers.

Ron belonged to a Catholic theatre group called the Cardijnian Players, where his fondness for dominance found an outlet in directing and writing. By 1951, when I thought there was modest evidence of literary ability, he was quick to put me straight. 'Your talent, I have to say, is for the cameo. I prefer the broad canvas and epic sweep.'

He soon got what he wanted. Ron was commissioned to write a play about the life of St Jean Baptiste de la Salle, founder of the order of Brothers at whose school he taught. The result, as described in *Conway's Way*, his self-serving memoir (is there any other kind?) was as follows: 'Suitably steeped in the history of 17th Century France, I wrote four huge acts, with nearly 40 speaking parts . . . the sheer scope of the play supports the conviction I've shared with the composer Vaughan Williams: "I have always preferred the imperfections of epics to the perfection of miniatures." '

Though there wasn't a single joke in *The Courtier of God*, it remains one of the funniest productions I've ever seen. Conway had dragooned some of his colleagues into performing. The sight of Desmond O'Grady trembling with terror as the French statesman Colbert, and other untidy Campion Society members in pantaloons and plumes mumbling their lines before a flouncing Louis XIV (played, inevitably, by the author) sent Bill Hannan and myself, safe in the back stalls, into convulsions.

There was a chorus, featuring the Women of France ('Lo! The fields of France lie golden in the sun, ripe for the harvest') but the high point came just before a keenly awaited interval. The curtain suddenly dropped, leaving de la Salle, who was seated on a chair having an attack of melancholia, marooned at the front of the stage. Though supposed to be near to tears, when he looked up and realised his predicament, he burst out laughing and propelled himself backwards though the drapes. In the front row, the heads of the distinguished hierarchy invited for the occasion bobbed up and down in something close to hysteria.

In the hope of saving me from what he saw as an impending crisis, Ron paid me a visit, and in our lounge room, with my brother giggling behind the door, formally offered me his friendship, and laid out a manifesto that was to govern it: mutual respect; a refusal to criticise the other behind their back; and a readiness to accompany the other on outings of a cultural nature. It sounded like an emotional contract, and produced in me a desire to flee. He was jilted, and our relationship cooled.

By the time the Campion Society had honed their distinctions, Vladimir Petrov had defected, the Industrial Groups had split the Labor Party, Menzies had won the 1954 election, and I had become a Bachelor of Arts (Pass).

The West St Kilda CYMS branch ignored the warnings of a Communist apocalypse and continued with their customary activities of drinking and sport. I now opened the batting for their cricket team. Our home ground was the mysteriously named Peanut Farm, behind Luna Park. A large crowd inexplicably attended our opening match, only to turn their backs in a reverse Mexican wave at regular intervals. The Farm was the headquarters of the local SP betting industry, and cricket gave them the perfect between-race pretext.

Cricketing standards were low, but there was a nine-gallon keg set up on the back of a utility as an incentive to dispose of the opposition quickly. When all else failed, as it often did, the captain would call on Maurie to send down his medium pacers. Maurie, a crimson-hued alcoholic, had a whirring windmill action that could shoot the ball at the close-in fieldsmen, the

Practising for the West St Kilda Catholic Young Men's Society football team.

batsman, and occasionally at the wicket. Once he whirled the ball so hard he bowled himself in the foot and had to be carried off.

Horrie, king of the chimps

Secondary studentships provided only a small living allowance, compelling me to show a range of incompetencies in part-time jobs: stuffing kapok into pillows (lasting one week), builders' labourer (four days, after falling down a manhole) and scrubbing thousands of ball marks off the walls of three squash courts at my father's club ('the exercise will do you good').

There was also the Titles Office, where there was casual work as a filing clerk. This involved climbing metal companionways to retrieve or return bulky folios of land titles, which gave up generations of dust when opened or closed.

The job attracted a variety of what were then called displaced persons. They included a gentle Hungarian intellectual called Tom Pick whose family had once had a sausage factory in Budapest. He was scholarly, owlishly bespectacled, and occasionally unintentionally patronising. 'What? You have read Apollinaire?' And Hans, who'd flown with the Luftwaffe and had seen 'terrible things'. He had a high nervous colour and always seemed on the verge of eruption. One morning, when we were enjoying our extended tea break high up on the catwalks, we heard a commotion below. Hans was having a fit on the floor. Something had triggered a wartime memory, and staff had to pinion his arms and legs as he lay there, crucified and screaming.

Work was undemanding at the Titles Office, and at the Melbourne Zoo almost non-existent. We were supposed to be painting the outdoor seats, but under the tolerant foremanship of an old ex-digger named Drummer, you could make yourself comfortable under one of them and doze off.

A fellow-worker, a portly and expensively tailored Bachelor of Education from one of the Gulf states, found the work demeaning. He had no intention of wedging himself under a seat, and opted for the revolving wheel in the playground. He'd stretch out on it, have us push him, and fall asleep. One afternoon the Works Manager appeared not long after we'd got him circling. He leaned over the rotund form and told him he was fired. He took his dismissal in style, allowing himself a couple more leisurely turns before easing himself onto the ground and, looking as ever the real manager in his well-cut beige suit, striding off.

More comedy followed the next day. 'Don't go near that chimp,' Drummer warned, 'he's a grumpy bastard.' As soon as Drummer disappeared for his morning smoko, we dared one another to go behind the safety fence and taunt Horrie. I did so, in front of a handful of visitors. I taunted it, glowering under its hessian sack. Then I threw gravel at it. Horrie hurled himself at me, shot an arm through the bars and grabbed at my jumper, while I performed an equally speedy move backward. I came out shamefaced, to laughter. 'If he'd a' got you,' said Drummer later, 'he'd a' broken your arm like a fucking carrot.'

So this is Darwin

The time I dreaded had now arrived – the post-graduate Diploma of Education year. To take our minds off it, Desmond O'Grady and I set out on a hitchhike to Darwin over the summer holidays. Every father needs something to hold up to his children about his youthful adventurousness. The now white-bearded and slippered patriarch, too young for World War II and too old for Korea or Vietnam, sometimes falls back on his second hitchhike: he too had once been at the hot gates.

In 1953 Darwin was a remote outpost, and to try to hitch there was regarded by our mothers as foolhardy and possibly dangerous. But Desmond was a doer, not a dreamer or a drinker. He would sometimes come to our Campion Society meetings. During evenings of what we thought were merriment and ribaldry, Desmond would sit over his glass of milk, unsmiling and unmoved.

If I was holding back in life because of shyness, Desmond was pushing forward, meeting editors, poets, professors and girls, getting stories published in *Melbourne University Magazine*. I was once in the study of Father Golden, the genial Newman Society chaplain, when he picked up a copy and said to Desmond: 'Starting to make a name for yourself, I see.' I felt wounded and out of it – literature as well as life.

This was my chance to catch up. *Newsweekly*, a strident Santamaria tabloid, had agreed to run my despatches on the adventure, only fragments of which, mercifully, remain: *We breathed deeply the cooler air. The morning was warm blue.*

We made good progress to Wangaratta and then Dubbo, and between Cobar and Wilcannia I had an experience (later to be inflicted on *Newsweekly* readers). Slim, the surly Cobar mailman, conveyed to us in the pub in a series of monosyllables that he wasn't allowed to carry passengers, but if we waited at 4 am at a spot 'a coupla miles outa town' he'd take us on to Wilcannia, for a fiver apiece.

We walked out of the copper-hard town at sunset, rolled out our sleeping bags and tried to get some sleep. I lay there unsleeping, while my friend snored, and looked up at the stars. The roof of the universe seemed to have been suddenly lowered, and looked brilliantly and tantalisingly close. As I confided to my readers: *I felt a strange doubleness. I was as near as I'd ever be to the mystery of things, two miles out of a town on the edge of the world. Overpowering centrality and marginality at the same time.*

At Wilcannia we were stuck for two days on the side of the road. The town had more crows per hectare of sky than anywhere we'd ever known. We were picked up by two men who'd spent all day in the hotel arguing over a woman, and who were comatose with drink. The driver kept falling asleep over the steering wheel, and we'd start to veer off the road. Desmond and I took turns leaning over from the back seat and doing the steering. We tacked all the way to Broken Hill.

At Quorn we gave up and caught the Ghan, which at the time took forty-eight hours to get to Alice Springs. There were first and second class and rough class, reserved for Aboriginal people and drifters like ourselves. At every stop there was a stampede over the sand to the pub. Men came back with hessian bags stuffed with bottles of beer and settled down to drink themselves insensible. Before he reached that stage, a lonely Finn went mad and came at us with a knife. We calmed him down, but after two sleepless nights on the jolting floor of the carriage I knew how he must have felt.

At Alice Springs we hitched another illegal ride on top of

a truck, shielding ourselves from the fierce December sun with our groundsheets and hats. Hundreds of miles later, somewhere past Daly Waters (where were the waters?) my hat blew off, and when I got down from the truck at Mataranka I fell to the ground raving. ('You were babbling about golden arrows going into your head,' said Desmond. 'Literary, even in delirium.')

After much grumbling about city idiots from the south, I was driven to Katherine by a tough guy in crocodile-skin boots who lit one cigarette off the butt of the one before. It took him a packet of Army Club to get me to hospital, where I was put in a ward with a ringer whose pride was the turn-the-match-flame-blue-with-a-fart trick. There was also an old prospector who refused to be washed. He had to be forcibly squirted with water, which set him yelling that the river was coming up and the crocs were going to get him.

SO THIS IS DARWIN trumpeted the *Newsweekly* headline, but it wasn't. I never got there. Desmond went on, noted

Deeply constipated on a round-Australia hitchhike, 1954.

what he saw, collected me on the way back, and with a little help from him and a few adjectives, I made Darwin up.

After further adventures, we found ourselves in central Queensland as Christmas approached. Near Biloela we managed to thumb down a train, and as we rattled through the outback we had an argument about the Symbolist Movement in French poetry. When we got off, constipated, sleepless and sick of one another, we squatted by the side of the road about a cricket pitch apart. I declared myself to be at the bowler's end, and reinforced my argument about Symbolism by pitching small stones at him. Desmond walked up from the batsman's end and started kicking me round the legs. While he kicked and I punched, a group of railway fettlers resting on a nearby fence shouted encouragement. 'What's up with youse blokes?' I imagined them saying. Our response would have been a puzzler: 'We're fighting about the Symbolist Movement in French poetry.'

Do you think he's normal?

None of these rigours gave me the slightest help in my quest for maturity and poise. Valerie had already noted the oddity of a Catholic taking her to see a Communist film at the New Theatre, and I had more in store. She agreed to come with me to a symphony concert at Melbourne Town Hall, in a tone that suggested this could be my last chance.

We arranged to meet under the portico, and to calm my nerves I had a couple of beers beforehand. Unable to say the words toilet or bathroom in her presence, I didn't go at interval.

The concert finished with Brahms's First Symphony. As the music built, so did the pressure on my bladder. The adagio – come on! The andante – get on with it! At last, the finale (which Brahms was accused of pinching from Beethoven). My companion's transported, while I'm about to explode. Will row five disappear in a golden shower? Would I have to rush out and suffer irretrievable loss of face? With only a couple of minutes to go, with crescendos thundering around me, I suddenly got up and pushed past endless knobbled knees to the exit. All the evidence was now in. Valerie was out with a madman.

Jane from my student teacher days had long gone elsewhere, but there was still the handsome Heather, my tormentor from behind the frosted glass. How to ask out the girl next door? Planning was needed. She lived with her aunt, so her car had to be out, and my mother had to be out too, and Heather had to be in.

Three planets had to be in alignment. When the time came, I took up the phone and dialled, and was so unmanned to hear it ringing next door that I put it down again. I took two nips of my father's whisky, dialled again, and heard it again, counterpointed by the high throbbing of my heart. Heather answered. I heard her voice on the phone and, distantly, off it as well.

'It's me,' I said, attempting insouciance, 'your next-door neighbour.'

She sounded interested: 'We haven't really met, have we?'

'What about the Alma Road bus stop in twenty minutes?'

'Okay.'

To avoid the absurdity of our both going up the street together to meet, I walked round the block. I was there, waiting, as she – to again Mills-&-Boon for a moment – swayed towards me, statuesque and smiling. The auguries were good.

Over the next few weeks we pooled (Olympic, Batman Avenue), pictured (*Attila the Hun*, with Jack Palance) and parked (Alma Reserve) – but why, she wondered, did we always meet at the designated place, and not go there together. It's hard to explain, I'd reply, because it was.

Our sunny relationship ended in the usual way – in embarrassment. One night I'd made the customary covert arrangement to meet Heather, this time outside the Town Hall, in the city ('You're seeing a lot of Dick Hughes,' my mother said – after I'd overheard her saying to my father, 'D'you think he's normal?'). I waited and waited, then gave up and went home. 'Heather rang from next door,' said my mother, in a voice in which hurt and triumphant discovery were mingled. 'She said she was sorry, but she couldn't make it tonight. She's not well.'

As her own marriage gradually failed, my mother had built up a powerful emotional relationship with me (and my brother), and as well as being hugely embarrassed, I felt I'd let her down. I'd let Heather down too. Why the secrecy? Why my mother's shock when she answered the phone? Was I ashamed of her? Why a man of twenty-three had to conceal a relationship with the attractive girl next door from his mother is something even now I can't fully explain – though Ron Conway would have been only too pleased to. The affair cooled and died.

Are you sure you're cut out for this?

February 1954 would not be put off: time for the Diploma of Education year to begin. I liked the safety of the lectures and dreaded when we were to put them into practice. My shyness was now forced out into the open. I had to face large groups of up to forty smirking adolescents and give them lucid, structured and lively lessons (the recommended adjectives).

I had only two defences: pills and alcohol. Oblivon had just come onto the market, and was only a vowel away from the desired state. The instructions on the packets stressed that only one should be taken initially, so before my first exposure to an English class I took two with difficulty: they were almost the size of toy footballs. On no account, the instructions went on, should alcohol be consumed while on this medication, so after getting them down I went over to a nearby hotel and had a couple of beers.

Something strange happened on my way back to Northcote High School: a highly bearable lightness of being. I sailed into the classroom, floated up to the platform, introduced myself with a deprecatory laugh, and said we'd now have a look at Alfred Noyes's *The Highwayman*.

At this stage in my literary life I'd cruised past T.S. Eliot and moved into Mayakovsky and Apollinaire, whose *Zone*, I insisted, was the great modern poem. *The Waste Land* was passé and the Georgians not worth considering. Each student was to read a portion, and as the couplets began their balladeering progress around the class, I began rocking backwards and forwards with the rhythm. As the metre got faster, so did I. When we reached the climax, with the highwayman riding unsuspectingly to his fate ('Tlot, tlot, tlot, tlot – had they heard it? The horse's hooves ringing clear') and the class laughing at me, the poem or both, gripped by a pharmaco/alcoholic fever, I held up a hand: 'Class,' I said, my notes about rhythm and rhyme forgotten, 'this is a silly poem. A romantic, melodramatic fool of a poem.' At this, Mr Brophy, the supervising teacher, got to his feet. 'Okay, class, Mr Oakley doesn't seem to like this poem, but I do, and tomorrow I'll tell you why.' Then the bell rang, and Brophy, grim-faced, waited for them to leave. He could manage only a single sentence: 'Are you sure you're quite cut out for this?'

I wasn't cut out for this, and a few weeks later I proved it. The school was the prestigious Melbourne High, and the teacher a short, irascible man called Baker. There'd be no nonsense here. Since mine was the final lesson of the morning, I forbore my medications, and in a state of pre-teaching terror got the runs instead. I fled to the student, not the staff lavatory, because it was closer. After I'd finished, the door refused to open. After some futile kicking and punching, I had no choice but to slide out underneath. What did the group of boys in 4B make of their visiting teacher suddenly presenting himself to them feet first, followed by an arm holding a briefcase?

Smirks and titters

At the beginning of February 1955, when England was winning the fourth test in Adelaide, and Tom Dougherty of the Australian Workers' Union claimed a secret society known as The Movement was trying to take control of the ALP, my father drove me in his pre-war Plymouth to the central Victorian town of Maryborough, to whose Technical School I had been posted by the Education Department. I had failed in Practical Teaching, and would have to complete my Diploma of Education later on.

Accommodation had been arranged by my fellow-Campion

Kevin Keating, who was teaching at the high school. I had a large room in a red-brick building that had once been a Mechanics' Institute, and was now Wandsworth, a warren of flats.

Kevin, who was destined for the Dominicans and who tried, usually in vain, to get me to go with him to daily Mass, offered to teach me how to drive his Vespa. One twilight, when I was at the controls, we went from sealed to unsealed surface on a back road. The front wheel wobbled and suddenly we were airborne. I hit the ground hard, suffering abrasions to fingertips and hip. We changed positions on the hardy Vespa, and Kevin took me to Maryborough Hospital, where I spent a week.

I was tended by a nurse's assistant of Amazonian proportions. She was big, but it was a shapely bigness, and when she offered to carry my suitcase home for me I accepted. And when I offered in turn to escort her home in the dark (who would have dared attack her?) she accepted.

The darkness improved her (and maybe me), and since we were both over six feet I didn't have to lean over for our lips to meet. My brother and I had once been fans of the wrestling at West Melbourne Stadium. We'd seen Dutch Hefner seize Chief Little Wolf in a bear hug, and I was likewise pinioned. After some close bodywork in which I got trapped against a gatepost, I freed myself and escaped.

Next day, when I bought my bread at the bakery, there was smirking and tittering as my loaf was wrapped, and I discovered when I returned to my room that the paper was covered in drawings. They showed, in a range of positions, a stick figure labelled 'Teecher' engaging with a girl the size of a zeppelin.

I'd learned my first lesson of country town life. The next day, the third form English class, all girls, broke into giggles as soon as I entered the classroom. The prefabs we taught in were walled with windows, and the windows gave onto the road. Not long after I'd calmed them down and announced we were going to have a look at conjunctions, a couple of dogs demonstrated their function on the footpath outside.

The windows were a mistake. Not much happened in Maryborough, and a lot of what did occurred in that particular street. There was the bolting horse incident; the peroxide blonde imbroglio ('Who wants to ride the town bike?' was whispered from boy to boy as she high-heeled past); the furniture van fiasco (when the back doors gave way and chairs and tables tumbled out); and the squeaky progress of Harry King and his son, their horse-drawn cart piled high with junk. They went past once a week, and the whole class would stand, turn to the window and salute.

But the road was handy for Bob Buttsworth, the head of the English Department (there were only the two of us). Bob, bustling, jovial and pencil-moustached, was quick to recognise he had a fellow malcontent. 'We've got to get out of this,' he'd say. His way out was a complex betting system ('The Graduate System', the advertisement proclaimed – 'Devised by a university academic.'). He did well out of it, at least for a while. For Bob, the road was perfect. He could slip out and listen to the mid-week races in his car. Apart from the horses, his other interest was his new black Holden. A row of cleaning cloths hung from his garage wall, with a label above each: Bonnet, Hubcaps, Boot, Mudguards, Windscreen. In the dim light, the trophy glowed.

I spent an occasional evening with Alf Berryman, a fellow inmate of Wandsworth. Alf was old and deaf and ran music classes, in front of whom he'd sometimes fall asleep after putting on a record. His morning departures for the school were one of the sights of the town. His vintage Riley gave out whirring death-ray noises when he started it up. Then he'd whine down the driveway and head straight onto the road, to angry tootings from cars he'd narrowly missed.

Most weekends I followed Bob Buttsworth's advice and took to the highway to Melbourne. Friday was sports day, so I could set off early in the afternoon and hitch a ride, often with commercial travellers, who'd sometimes insist on calling in to hotels on the way – drinking from Castlemaine to Kyneton to Diggers' Rest. You could drink after hours if you were that legal fiction, a bona fide traveller, and signed a book to this effect. For the rest of the Victorian population, hotels still closed at six.

In amoral New South Wales, six o'clock closing was abolished in 1955, but Victorians had to wait another ten years, perpetuating one of the great frontier spectacles – the dynamo roar of the Young and Jackson's drinkers as closing time approached, the lining up of beers as last drinks were called, and the stumbling of drunken men across Flinders Street to the station afterwards.

Dead

One April morning, Mrs Gillies, the landlady, knocked on my door to say there was an urgent phone call for me. I took it in her panelled lobby, every detail of which still remains clear to me, in the light-flash of the news. It was Lorna Hogan. Terry Mahony, one of our closest friends, had died in hospital, from a gunshot wound, after a long night at a Newman Society ball.

Terry had gone back with Bill Ginnane (another friend,

though less close) to Ginnane's house. There was a rifle in the spare bedroom where he was recuperating. Somehow it had gone off, fatally wounding Terry. That was all Lorna knew. She was in shock and so was I. Terry had been one of the Newman Society stars, a graduate in law, now working for his father's firm of solicitors, but his real interests were theological. He knew his Aquinas, and while we waffled, he would have the exactly-right Thomist quote. I'd known him at school, had played cricket and football with him, drank and argued with him, and now he was dead.

There was an Irish vigil at the Mahony house on the Friday: a night of prayers around an open coffin. I didn't go. I simply couldn't imagine him waxen and inert, arms folded across his chest. The Requiem Mass and funeral followed on the Saturday morning, and I felt the weight of him as we shouldered him to his grave.

There was grief, puzzlement and then questions: a rifle in the bedroom had somehow discharged. There was nothing in the respectable dailies, but *Truth*, the Melbourne scandal sheet, was right onto it: 'Solicitor shot dead. Secret police probe' was the front-page lead a week later. 'Homicide detectives who have been conducting a hush-hush probe into the tragedy have been unable to find out how he was wounded.'

Four months later there was an inquest, and again *Truth* was the only paper to cover it. 'Hush hush death' was the headline, and it got worse: 'Someone, somewhere, has been trying ever since to hush up the whole affair. Now the coroner's court has made an "open" finding, but how and why Terence Mahony was fatally wounded remains a mystery.

'Ginnane said that he had returned to the kitchen and had been reading the paper when he heard a noise from the room, and Mahony's only words to him were "Bill, Bill, I'm shot – get a doctor". Senior Detective Carton testified that he could not find any suspicious circumstances, nor any reason why Mahony would commit suicide (he was engaged to an attractive young woman and his legal career was going well).

'But', *Truth* added, 'further evidence, which may have assisted the coroner to reach a definite conclusion, was not before him. In an official file there is a statement from Dr John Francis, who saw Mahony in hospital. Dr Francis said he asked another doctor in front of Mahony if the shooting was accidental. Mahony shook his head, indicating that it was not. Yet he was not called upon to give evidence.

'This is further complicated by the fact that Ginnane had earlier said that he was "sitting up in bed having a cup of tea when he heard a noise". This inconsistency was never questioned – nor the fact that Mahony lingered for a day in hospital but gave no one an account of what had happened.'

Since Bill Ginnane, who went on to become Reader in Philosophy at the Australian National University, is now dead, it seems that the mystery of Terry's death, and of the inadequacy of the inquest, will never be solved – despite the effort of Lorna Hannan (née Hogan), who unearthed much of the above material, and who loved him as a friend, as did I and many others. Maybe it's better to have no closure. Then things remain open, and in that mystery Terry Mahony still lives.

Two boys

As the grinding-wheel wore on – hitchhikes in the winter cold, the daily battle to maintain order and interest – I longed for escape, but not in the way of Jim Kennedy. Kennedy, porridge-pale and melancholy, taught at the high school with Kevin Keating, and it was Keating who broke the news to me.

'Jim Kennedy's on a morals charge,' he said, as we shared a late-afternoon bottle of beer. 'The cops came and took him away. He's just been released. I've invited him round.'

'A morals charge?'

'Two boys.'

We sat down to eat our nightly grilled chops and three veg, listening for footsteps on the stairs. Soon we heard them, then the knock on the door.

Jim Kennedy's Celtic paleness had changed to grey, as if he'd suddenly turned sixty. No thanks, he wasn't hungry. He sat in the single shabby armchair and stared ahead. The silence seemed unbreakable.

'What'll you do?' Kevin managed.

'Go. Tomorrow's train. Go.'

Two boys. With one he'd have a chance, but not with two.

'D'you have a drink?'

'That was our last beer. Sorry.'

Kennedy got up and scanned the mantelpiece. There were bottles of various shapes, all empty. Except one: Dolly Varden Wine Cocktail, inherited from the previous tenant.

'You can't drink that. No one can drink that.'

'Always a first.'

He poured himself a glass. It was an unpleasant brownish colour, thick and syrupy.

'My hemlock,' he said. He managed half a glass, then shook our hands and left.

I had a period off the next day about the time the train was due, and walked up to the station. The Melbourne platform stretched into the distance and at the far end, past families, two old ladies and a porter having a smoke, under a turned-down hat, in a turned-up overcoat, was Kennedy, with a single case. Should I? Reluctantly I headed down the platform's great length. Kennedy was looking straight ahead, at the large MARYBOROUGH sign across the tracks. When he registered – I was on gravel now – he picked up his case and walked straight past me, as if I wasn't there.

Lovely girls – and literature

At least he'd escaped. So had Desmond O'Grady the year before, by persuading a psychiatrist that Maryborough was bad for his mental health. I agreed with him, but no psychiatrist was going to free me from the three-year bondage to the Education Department (they'd paid my university fees).

Worse – the town I was trapped in, one of a cluster of old goldrush settlements in Central Victoria – was disappearing before my eyes. The shire council had decided that the main street needed a makeover. The old shop verandahs that gave the place its character were removed, and Maryborough became soulless and suburban. In the fifties, to conserve was a word solely applied to jam.

Then Kevin Keating announced he was moving out too – but only to Ararat, where he'd been transferred. In December, two of his ex-students, now at Bendigo Teachers' College, came to say goodbye to him. They knocked on his door, and when it wasn't answered went inside (he never locked his door – 'What can they pinch?' he'd say). Kevin had been a creative teacher, and they showed they were too by decorating his room with palm leaves ripped from a tree outside my window, while I cowered inside, wondering what the landlady would think.

When Kevin got home, he called me upstairs to meet Rosemary Temple (short and dark) and Carmel Hart (tall and golden-haired). His monastic flat had become a greenroom, with fronds fanning up from fireplace, windows and walls. 'Lovely girls,' Kevin said as we were introduced. (It was his generic term for all young women.)

When they were leaving, I followed the lovely girls down the stairs, held onto the handlebars belonging to the taller one and asked what she was doing over the Christmas holidays. She said she'd be in Melbourne. I said I would be too. And here we go again:

'Perhaps we could . . . at some stage while you were there . . .'

'Meet?' That was the word I was after, but she looked like Botticelli's Venus and my legs looked skinny in my baggy shorts. 'Perhaps I could . . .' Venus waited patiently for the punch line – 'Give me a ring? I don't have the number. I'm staying with a friend.' (A boyfriend, what else?)

Knowing I had no hope, I battled on. 'Could I give you mine, then?' (Don't call us, we'll call you.) She wrote it down, and then floated away, as if the bicycle was airborne.

Every day during that long summer, I hoped for a call. And if she did ring, I worried, she might get my mother. 'Barry? You want Barry? Who am I speaking to?'

Uncalled, I sought distraction in literature. Encouraged by

the publication of a short story in an ephemeral literary magazine called *Direction* (four issues) I wrote another, about Burke and Wills, which took as long to appear in *Southerly* as the duo did to cross the continent.

Desmond O'Grady, friend and rival, was matching me – he too was in *Direction* (he was associate editor, so he got himself in twice in the opening issue, one under the unlikely pseudonym of James Desmond) and in *Southerly* too.

We were together in prose, and together in drama. Earlier in the fifties we'd seen Lorca, Ben Jonson and Sophocles at the tiny Arrow Theatre in South Melbourne, run by (and whenever possible starring) Frank Thring – the only camp Oedipus I've ever seen. Verse drama was the fashionable mode. We were dazzled by Christopher Fry's *The Lady's Not for Burning*, bored by T.S. Eliot's *Murder in the Cathedral*, and prepared to suspend enough disbelief to accept gangsters speaking in verse (Maxwell Anderson's *Winterset*) – with the genre put under greatest strain in Douglas Stewart's *Ned Kelly*, as performed at the university's Union Theatre. When Felix Raab as Ned fell with a crash, his pentameters roaring trapped around his helmet, pathos became bathos, and muted titters could be heard.

There had to be another way, and in Australia it was Ray Lawler who found it. At the end of 1955, when the phone had stayed silent and hope abandoned, I saw *Summer of the Seventeenth Doll*, and witnessed a revelation – not in the play's form (a conventional three-acter) but in what Lawler had done with it. Here were working-class characters speaking gruff working-class language, but when Lawler put an electrical charge through it, its very resistance made the words glow like a filament.

There were gasps of audience recognition as the rough

language poured out – not of themselves but of the working-class types who, in those days, still lived in Carlton. Frissons swept through us as we heard forbidden words – bastard, bloody, bugger – that only seven years before, in Sumner Locke Elliott's *Rusty Bugles*, had to be changed, under threat of prosecution, to stinker, mug and dimwit.

Vincent's Powders

hen it was back to Maryborough. I took over Kevin Keating's flat, and Brian Sharp, a fellow teacher and friend, moved into my old room below. He soon had inmates complaining of what Mrs Gillies called 'that awful music'. It was Sibelius, and he taught me to revere him (I could hear it upstairs). I went to Melbourne less often, and plunged into Proust.

On Friday 23 November, distant Melbourne suddenly came up close. 'IT'S AFLAME.' That was the *Sun News Pictorial* banner headline, with the rest of the front page showing the runner Ron Clarke squinting into the sparks and smoke as he carried the Olympic torch into the Melbourne Cricket Ground. Despite the concerns of the Olympic supremo Avery Brundage, Melbourne had made it on time and was famous for the Warholian number of days.

A huge inflated kangaroo floated above the city, with a giant pink Aspro packet sticking up from the pouch. When the wind blew it moved in rhythmic thrusts, as if mythically engendering the spectacle beneath.

Tickets had gone quickly, and I could only manage one to the heavyweight boxing, in which a fair-haired, fast-moving

Russian danced around an acromegalic Bulgarian giant for four rounds before he did a King Kong collapse onto the canvas. It was the exact opposite of what was going on in Europe, where the Russians had invaded Hungary to put down a revolt against Communist rule.

The revolt was crushed, but the battle continued when the two countries met in the water polo. There was blood in the water when the game was halted by the referee. Hungary was leading, and was credited with a victory, and went on to win the gold medal. Half the Hungarian delegation refused to go back.

Until November 1956, a Berlin Wall of provincialism surrounded Melbourne. The Games broke it open, and television, which had just arrived, poured through the gap. We stood at electrical shop windows to watch Bruce Gyngell usher it in. He was in a dinner suit, and behind him were packets of Vincent's Aspirin Powders arranged to form the letters TV. The symbolism was perfect.

The findings of the Royal Commission set up before television was introduced sound like something from the Dead Sea Scrolls. 'The objective from the outset must be to provide programmes that would have the effect of raising standards of public taste. The danger is that success depends on an appeal to numbers, and it is difficult to escape mediocrity and vulgar sensationalism.' 'Vulgar' now sounds dated and snobbish, but that's what most television now is: the V in TV.

Funny eyes

In December 1956, with the school year closing and me secretly planning to join Desmond O'Grady in Rome, the teachers had a wind-up dinner. I managed the stairs quite well afterwards, opened my door, and Carmel Hart's sitting in the shabby armchair by the window – the girl who wouldn't ring, the girl who sailed past in the main street in her red-haired boyfriend's car (acknowledging me with a wave).

'What were you wearing?' I ask her, fifty-four years later. I couldn't remember, and she couldn't either. And *why* was she there? (Even now I can't really figure it out.) She was back from Bendigo Teachers' College, had had a row with her parents, and since she'd broken up with her boyfriend, when she walked out of her house she had nowhere to go.

So I was visited, it seemed, by default. Though what had attracted her, she later told me, was her father's opinion of me after he'd done some repairs at Wandsworth. He had heard me talking to myself on the landing: 'He's mad.'

After some awkward groping-for-common-ground talk, Carmel Hart said she'd better be going. But where? That was okay – she could climb back through a window. 'I'll walk you home then.' (Confidence at last!) Instead of farewells at her front gate on the outskirts of town, we agreed they could be better done beside the fenced paddock opposite. It was a summer's night, the moon was up, we looked, we gazed, and in the words of one of Joseph Heller's novels, Something Happened. Falling in love is not only corny, but wrong. It's a soaring, with each responding to the other the way birds do, when they court in the air.

When we'd come down to earth I saw her to her gate, said

goodbye and, feeling as if I were floating several feet above the ground, left. Five minutes later Carmel Hart was running after me. Her father had locked the window; she couldn't get in. Since my fellow lodger Brian Sharp had now left for Melbourne, I installed her chastely in his room for what was left of the night.

In Europe the town focus is the square; in Australian country towns in summer it's the swimming pool. During Maryborough's unsparing winters, the pool was no more than a white scoop of concrete, dormant behind the trees of the park. In September it was watered back to life, and by November the whole town seemed to gather round it, like Hindus by the Ganges, celebrating rebirth. We joined in the celebrations, and had a courtship in and out of the water, submarine and ultramarine.

After romance, ritual. I met her parents, we had the requisite cups of tea and lamingtons, and Carmel declared it a success. Her father Harry hadn't found me mad after all, though her mother Anne said that I had 'funny eyes'. Then it was her turn. Aunts and uncles and family friends were arranged around our lounge room, and my mother wheeled in her big-occasion auto tray, laden with more than lamingtons – Alexanders from Patersons of Chapel Street, cream cakes, vanilla slices and a crowning sponge – crushingly middle-class hospitality, perhaps designed to put rural inferiors in their place. My mother called Carmel 'dear' a lot, and though Carmel later said it felt like a Royal Show judging, this too was declared a success. My mother later agreed, though having heard of Anne's opinion that I had funny eyes, she riposted that while Carmel was a lovely girl, her legs were a little large.

We became engaged, as one did then, very soon after. It was concentrically celebrated with two parties at Carmel's South

Caulfield flat. There were balloons and booze, but no interactions between my university friends and her Bendigonians, who soon went outside and began running around the house bellowing pop songs, while the intellectuals huddled in the living room singing the then-fashionable psalms of the French composer Joseph Gelineau. At the inner party Carmel encountered puzzled stares (how did *he* get *her*?) and at the outer earlier suitors, now well away, threatened to carry her off and save her from these hymn-singing wimps.

Who chose his trousers? (I'm now engaged to Carmel.)

Man and wife

So instead of a ship to Italy with my friend Bill Hannan, I took a night train with my new fiancé to Mildura, where we'd both been posted, to alight dazed at 6 am at Ouyen for refreshments in preparation for the final unsteady leg – because, we were told, the desert sand doesn't provide a firm foundation for the tracks.

Mildura might have been remote but its population was surprisingly mixed. As well as pastoralists and blockies (grape growers) in wide flat hats, there were Italians, Greeks, Slavs, bodgies, pig-hunters, ferals, Aboriginal people and drifters. A few days later a Hungarian refugee train further enriched the mix (they were from the failed uprising two months earlier). We were paying a Saturday visit to the Catholic church when it began to fill up with them, with United Nations Refugee Organisation in white letters on their brand-new bags. They processed up the aisle behind a priest in gold vestments, and chorused responses to his intonations of lament or thanksgiving. (Where in the hell have we ended up? they must have wondered.)

To avoid temptation we took rooms at a chaste distance. The Education Department solved the problem by declaring Carmel 'surplus to requirements' and exiled her temporarily to a place even more remote – Manangatang, where the big event, she told me, after coping with the culture shock, was the arrival of the weekly Melbourne train.

In the May term holidays we married, at St Mary's East St Kilda, with my old school friend Gerrard Briglia the celebrant. There was giggling amongst some of Carmel's relations at the little gong the altar boy bonged at the Nuptial Mass's consecration. We still have a brief colour movie of the couple leaving the church afterwards, in which Carmel looks dazedly beautiful and the groom is pulling strange faces – perhaps because we were both sedated on Oblivon, the unswallowable calmative that had got me through my Diploma of Education year.

The reception was to be at swish 9 Darling Street, but financial stringencies forced us to cross this out on the wedding invitation and replace it with the less-fashionable Esplanade

Bride and groom, sedated by the primitive tranquilliser Oblivon. May, 1957.

Hotel. As we arrived, Ted, the man who used to deliver butter to my grandmother and whom she inexplicably married (her second time), broke away from the welcoming guests, produced a ten-shilling note with a conjurer's flourish and put it in my hand. 'Keep it,' he said loudly. (Ted was as mean as he was ugly. When we visited them later with little children, he'd take off the tops of the garden taps so they wouldn't waste water.)

My brother drove us afterwards to a Warburton guesthouse, where we lasted only one night. The bed was uncomfortable and kids ran up and down the corridors too excited to go to sleep. The following morning, I complained to the manager. He was a rural humourist, accustomed to mocking honeymoon couples.

'Sleep?' he said. 'You're on your honeymoon, and you got no sleep?'

'That's right. We didn't get any.'

'You didn't get any, and you're complaining?'

'You're not getting any either. We're leaving.'

'You booked in for a week.'

'You've got the deposit, and that's all you're getting – though there might be more – on the sheets.'

We moved to a nearby hotel, where our trials continued. After our second night, Carmel broke out in giant hives. When I appeared at the highly public breakfast, and naively gave the reason for her absence, the news went round the tables and caused general merriment. 'Bad news, son,' said one bucolic wit. 'Looks like she's allergic to it.' Like mothers-in-law, honeymoon couples were comic figures. Ripostes were impossible.

Dutiful Catholics

We began married life in a flat in Thirteenth Street. Presumably the Chaffey brothers brought the idea of numbered streets from America, with the irrigation system on which Mildura is based. Every morning I'd ride my bike along Deakin Avenue to the Technical College, and Carmel would ride hers to Mildura Central.

Snob that I was, I'd hide in my little office at lunchtime and read copies of *Current Affairs Bulletin* on Wittgenstein or The Modern Novel. We'd both get home tired – so many kids, so much heat. On Friday night this would escalate to an argument over the shopping and washing, after which we'd go to the Rendez Vous, the town's only restaurant, enjoy freshly caught Murray cod and Mildara riesling, and share the latest schoolboy howlers with our friends Geoff Richards and Jack

Thomas: 'After the Romans had defeated all the countries they grew lazy and ate about a six-course meal and were defeated so their Empire fell.' Gibbon in a sentence.

We seemed to exert a powerful attraction upon lonely bachelors. The first of what would prove to be many was James McGrath, with whom I taught. James's only company, apart from us, were adolescent boys. Here was a man who could transfix a school assembly, yet who spent his spare time taking favourites to the movies, or leading one gang against another. We came to live in fear of him. In drink he'd lie on the floor, mouth agape, lips furled like a donkey's, declaring his great love for Carmel, and taking umbrage when finally asked to leave. 'But I *live* here.'

We were dutiful Catholics at the time. Every Sunday we endured the pulpit polemics of Father Carroll, tall, bony and intense. 'Get this into your Catholic heads,' he'd bellow. 'While we fish and we swim and we go on drives, the Communists are taking over the unions.'

He came to the school to give Religious Instruction, and locked onto me. He called on us one night, dispensed with the civilities, and said he wanted to form a study group for the professional men of the town. I knew what was coming. 'A united front, that's what we need.' Calling on my years of dialectical experience with the Campion Society, I told him I was against united fronts.

'Ah,' he said, 'you're one of these individualists.'

'And intend to remain so.'

'I'm disappointed. You could be a great help to us.' I knew what he meant by that 'us'. It was a Movement word, a Santamaria word. For us or against us. He refused another beer and left. Never one to waste an experience, I based a piece of fiction on it later which went, via *Southerly*, into *The Oxford Book of Australian Short Stories*.

Teaching was closing in on me. The principal, the egregiously misnamed Mr Witty, decided it was time I took some responsibility and put me in charge of the bike racks, and I had to address the assembly regularly on the state of them. There were also staff meetings, to thrash out such matters as whether teachers should have to shut the windows after school, and whether qualifications should be added to names of staff listed in the school magazine.

Newly married, at Mildura Technical College, 1957. (I'm the happy one in the middle, top row.)

Escape! Attempts to do so by applying for positions in Manila and Japan failed. My first novel – inevitably about a teacher in a country town – was rejected, with red wine stains on some of my purplest passages. It was sent off twice more, and back it came each time, by now on the point of disintegration.

With pathways to literature and travel blocked, I applied to return to Melbourne. The Education Department had a way of dealing with those desperate to get back to the city. They'd be sent to the toughest schools: Collingwood, South Melbourne, Richmond. I was given Richmond, and the hardest year of my life.

Don't be nice

On my first day at Richmond Technical School, as we came down the stairs to the quadrangle, the kids booed. 'You can forget about your Diploma of Education,' said the head of the English Department. 'It's war, and you have to win it. Have you got a strap?' I said I hadn't. 'Get one from the office,' he said, as we lined up in front of the still-booing kids. 'Don't be nice.'

I hadn't mastered not being nice, and had to use other means. The toughest class was 3CD – forty leather-jacketed adolescents who didn't want to be there. They didn't want Dickens or Wordsworth, so I read from John O'Grady's *They're a Weird Mob*. If this was English literature they liked it, revelling in Jeez and bludge and 'flat as Aunt Maude's chest'. Things were okay as long as they were entertained, so in the football season I told them to buy the *Sporting Globe*. They were all Richmond supporters. Every Monday we'd read and discuss the prose of the hacks who described Richmond's match. They soon learned what clichés meant, and developed a skill in spotting them. Language badly used can be as instructive as its opposite.

In the classroom across the corridor, the war was being lost. The teacher, Livio, a gloomy Italian with an unwise moustache, spent the time either shouting at the class or riding the waves of noise that followed, with the noise eventually winning. 'I cannot go on like this,' he said. He didn't, and left.

Further along the corridor was the opposite: a totally silent class, ruled by a Mr Trevaskis. Mr Trevaskis was short but solid, and gave off a whispery menace, to such effect that he'd sometimes walk out and leave the class, and still there'd be quiet. I once witnessed a strapping when passing his room. He ran at his victims, to gain extra momentum. It happened only rarely.

My classes veered between order and chaos, with occasional recourse to the strap. Like the offender, I found this deeply unpleasant, but the problem was eventually solved for me. Someone had used their break-and-enter skills to get into my locked desk. The strap, each time I used it, seemed slightly shorter – it was done subtly, a couple of centimetres at a time. After a few weeks, my defensive armament was a harmless little leather flap.

There was only one strategy left. I collected a stack of *Walkabout* travel magazines from the library, and at difficult times gave them out. Suddenly, they'd go quiet. The search was on, I soon realised, for tribal articles that showed bare-breasted women. If erotica couldn't be found, the kids were happy to supply it. I thought they were busy taking notes, but what they were in fact doing was decorating almost every photograph – of man, woman, kangaroo, even aeroplane – with outsize male genitalia.

At Richmond I met my first genuine bohemian (if that's not a contradiction in terms). Jason Gurney taught art at the school, and he'd throw lumps of wet plaster at troublemakers instead of using the strap. Gurney was a large man who wore a shabby corduroy jacket and matching trousers. He had long greying hair, a goatee, a black beret and purple bags under his eyes. In profile he looked like Paul Gauguin.

I used to have morning tea with Gurney in his little office (he despised the other teachers) until I grew tired of being told that Melbourne was a provincial outpost, and that next year, as soon as he'd saved the money, he'd be back in Paris, London or New York. But if he'd had successful exhibitions in these places, if he knew Dylan Thomas and Ezra Pound, what was he doing here, under the plaster apples, with his Gauloises and airmailed copies of *New Statesman*? The answer, I eventually realised, was that he needed insularity, it was where he showed up best – where would he be in Paris with his beret and beard?

I went to one of his parties, in his studio, a converted stable behind St Kilda Road. He greeted guests in a red roar of a waistcoat and paint-flecked pants. He'd assembled a crowd of painters, phonies and poseurs, and looking down on them were his paintings, vacuous abstracts, blank and banal.

Jason Gurney wasn't very good, and this was why I witnessed one of the greatest snubs of all time. One afternoon, when I was having a drink with him after school, he noticed someone, a dark, handsome, bearded man, across the counter in the saloon bar. 'That's Clem Meadmore,' he said, 'you must meet him.' He called out to him, in a voice more and more plaintive – 'Clem – Clem – Clem . . .' Clem kept his eyes down as he got his drink. 'Clem!' There was as much steel in Clem as there was in his chairs, and he paid for his drink and turned away as if he were stone deaf.

By the middle of this exhausting year, when Carmel was pregnant, we'd extricated ourselves from my mother's house. ('Go on, take a flat. Your father's never here and Gavan's on the other side of the world, but I'll manage.') We moved into a place in Caulfield, where we could begin proper married life, and which Carmel furnished with a table, buffet and chairs in the new Scandinavian style. Melbourne was taking the first steps towards civilisation, and so were we. Every afternoon after work, pale and tired, I'd change into bottle-green corduroy trousers, settle into a Fler chair, and sip a Coonawarra claret.

We'd had a hectoring cleric in Mildura, and now we endured another at our local church in Caulfield. Father Gleeson was an Irish priest of the old and thankfully declining school, built like a bull with a roar to match, regularly inveighing against the modern world and predicting its eventual collapse. The birthrate would decline because of antisocial methods of contraception, and we'd be overwhelmed by more fecund races – including, presciently enough, those of Muslim faith. At one performance he was fulminating about contraception's evil when he was interrupted by a crying child. He stopped and waited, and the infant howled on. 'Either I go or that child goes,' he roared. The child went, enabling Gleeson to continue about the blessings of large families. And then we went, and didn't come back.

Birth and afterbirth

At about this time of exhausting class warfare, Bill Hannan and Desmond O'Grady, newly sophisticated, returned from Paris and Rome respectively. They wore sharp jackets and pointed shoes, and had bad news. Australia was not a good place for would-be novelists. Cultural thinness. Fiction couldn't grow in it. Bill went further. Not only did Australia have no soul, it wouldn't matter if it had. He'd converted to the French New Realists – Michel Butor and Alain Robbe Grillet, who maintained that fiction didn't need story or character, merely neutral descriptions of the external world: all that could be known was the surface of things.

Since I at the time was having a Ned Kelly period, and writing a story of his final hours which *Southerly*, moving at its own marmoreal pace, would eventually accept, I riposted by saying that Australia mightn't yet have a civilisation but it did have myths, and until cultivation and Left Bank berets came along they would do. All this was tossed back and forth as we wandered the suburban streets with the unavailability of a bar or coffee shop proving their point.

If Desmond was critical of Australian society he was surpassed by his Italian wife Gegi, whom he'd married in St Peter's in Rome. Both Gegi and Carmel were pregnant, and Carmel became a complaints sounding board. They ranged from the poverty of the cuisine to the lack of central heating. We had a party in our flat to welcome the visitors back to the land they weren't happy with, and the two pregnant wives found they were wearing identical coat-dresses from exclusive Georges. Though Carmel's was lilac and Gegi's light brown, she and Desmond left immediately.

By now the baby was imminent, and kicked at night as if impatient to get out. It made its escape early on the eighth of November, but seemed to have second thoughts beforehand, forcing Carmel to endure a thirty-six-hour labour. Her husband was not on hand to help. At our arrival at the hospital, we were confronted by a fierce nun, who told me to leave at once. The patient was briskly instructed to 'go and empty your bladder'.

Carmel was then taken into a cramped and primitive labour ward, with two beds separated only by a plastic sheet. As she endured her own labour, she had to listen to the cries of the woman on the other side as she gave birth, and then witness the doctor emptying the afterbirth into a basin. The hospital was called Bethlehem, and the name was apt.

When, after a day and a half, the baby arrived, she was blue, and taken away immediately. Her mother had to lie there uncleaned for hours, while others waited their turn on trolleys in the corridor. We called her Madeleine, and she had perfect features. 'When your father saw you after you were born,' my mother said helpfully, 'he went out and vomited.' We marvelled at this being that had begun life no bigger than a full stop at the end of a sentence. To hold that evolutionary accident was the sole cause of this miracle requires a leap of faith greater than that required for Christian belief. Madeleine was not the blind product of the forces of nature but a gift.

All done the old-fashioned way: first the wedding, then the baby (Madeleine).

The gift cried a lot at night, and every morning I'd emerge from our flat as if dazed by a dart and walk to Caulfield Technical College, to which I'd mercifully been transferred. Though the students were more manageable, teaching was just as trying as at Richmond. It was hard to be enthusiastic about punctuation in front of a class of forty after a run of sleepless nights.

Madeleine was soon getting teeth and I was losing them. The trouble went as far back as the war, when our father, who was in charge of Air Force stores on Thursday Island, sent us back a huge tin of quarter-pound blocks of chocolate. First we used them to build ships and castles, then we began eating them. After this, and a daily diet of lemon tarts in my school lunch, my teeth gradually succumbed, and I was forced to go to a dentist.

'They'll have to come out I'm afraid,' he said, as he inspected the stumps and stalactites of my upper jaw. A few days later, in a surgery opposite Caulfield Railway Station, a mask was put over my face, and I was told to inhale. It was nitrous oxide, laughing gas, and I had an Experience. I was ballooned to Somewhere Else, where the ace of diamonds had inexplicably to be presented to gain admittance to a behind-the-mirrorland quite different from the field of dreams. Things happen in dreams, but this was suspended in timelessness. I was floating in an eternal now, and this, it was immediately evident, was what the afterlife was going to be like. Time and space will fall away, leaving just you, treading presentness as one does water. You don't expect intimations from your dentist, but this has stayed with me ever since.

Nightmare of the red room

Despite her now having an indentured husband, Carmel was pregnant again, and we moved from the Caulfield flat to a characterless house in Carnegie, a characterless suburb. The price ($6500) was all we could afford. 'Stylish' was how the estate agent puzzlingly described it, and stylish was what Carmel did her best to make it become.

Some things needed doing in its progress towards this condition, and I couldn't do them. I was the kind of man who thought grout was the name of an Australian wicketkeeper, a bastard file a public service expletive, nogging something done with eggs, and sarking a Scottish folk dance. When the fuses went, we had to wait in the dark for my father to come, as he did when the pilot light went out under the hot-water tank.

Determined not to give up, I got up a ladder once to unscrew a curtain rod bracket. The screw had been painted over, and was immovable. At that moment one of Carmel's sisters and her husband arrived from Queensland. Alex, huge-handed and practicality incarnate, got up on the ladder, poked with the screwdriver and loosened the screw in what seemed one continuous movement. Alex was the kind of man who spent hours in his shed playing with tenon saws, mitre boxes and diaphragm valves.

When our second, Justin, arrived, he was brought into a house held together with Blu-Tack. He was a crier too, but we had three bedrooms now, so he could be consigned to the far end of the house. The bedrooms soon filled with a third and a fourth. On the arrival of the fifth, the lounge was taken over, which left us with only the kitchen and living room. By the time the quintet was put to bed with their bottles, books, teddies, dolls and blankets, this room was a wall-to-wall litter of toys. Every night we shoved them into cupboards, and every day they came back again. It was a pointless but essential ritual, a brief respite from detritus as relentless as lava.

We bought a Guernica print to put over the fireplace, and sometimes, on wet days, when the five were at play, war or both, Picasso's images of chaos and uproar reflected what was happening at floor level. The contrast between day and night became unsettling. Hours of shouts, thumps and howlings – and then, by eight o'clock, after the last story had been told, the last warning issued, silence. We'd sit with a glass of what was still called claret and at about half past ten open the door, creep down the hallways to the front bedroom, lie there and wait for sleep, knowing that when it came it was preparing to leave at least one of the children.

We had twelve years of broken nights, an endless catacomb of cryings and coughings, that focused particularly on what we called the red room. It had cheap red lino and a red night-light,

Married life in Carnegie.

and when going in there to a child trapped in a dream-terror, you seemed caught up in it too – the glow of ambulances and brothels, the nightmare redness in the heart of the dark. They might have been the swinging sixties for some. For us, they were the sleepless ones.

There is a scene in *Pride and Prejudice* where the wealthy and eligible Mr Bingley is seen unexpectedly approaching on his horse, sending the Bennet family running around in crazed circles. Our own reaction, when our leisure was precious, was similar. Is it Uncle Len from Newcastle? Auntie Gladys from Shepparton? Max the mad Fitzroy poet? At an unexpected knock, we'd shepherd the brood into the laundry and hide.

One lonely bachelor friend – we always had one lonely bachelor friend – used to outwit us by coming round the back, so we put a dustbin against the side gate as an early warning system. Once we heard it move, five little children had to be hidden and hushed. Finally the problem solved itself. One of the kids peeped out a window just as he was looking in, and he went away for good.

Every weekend, our boisterous household was rivalled by our next-door neighbours – an elderly couple and their middle-aged son. They lived in a state of passive alcoholism during the week and broke out on Saturday, pursuing one another from room to room while roaring insults. Next to them was another middle-aged misfit son who lived with his mother and went on peeping expeditions on summer nights. And next to them again lived a large, sullen Slavonic man who stared out at the world from his front gate and rarely went beyond it. One night he shuffled in his slippers to the railway line at the end of the street and was killed at the pedestrian crossing. Carnegie was not as characterless as I first thought.

Responsibility avoided again

In 1960 Brian Kiernan, absurdly youthful and freshly graduated MA from the University of Melbourne, arrived at Caulfield and we found much in common. It was a friendship built on books and a lunchtime beer.

Brian and his partner Suzanne moved into an Italianate mansion called Labassa. It has since been taken over by the National Trust, but was then divided into grand but shabby apartments. Theirs took in a drawing room and ballroom, and sometimes we had dinner there. We'd dine on the ballroom's podium, with a distant fire burning in the baronial grate, flickering highlights in the wallpaper's gold.

To add to its decaying glamour, Joe Lynch, the alcoholic subject of Kenneth Slessor's *Five Bells*, once lived in Labassa's tower:

Everything had been stowed
Into this room – 500 books all shapes
And colours dealt across the floor
And over sills and on the laps of chairs.

During the sixties, Brian's essays on such canonical novelists as Joseph Furphy, Xavier Herbert, Christina Stead and Patrick White rescued them from the benign prison of the democratic nationalist tradition, locating them within the vivifying currents of European and American fiction instead.

These essays, when collected into a book, also rescued Brian himself. They led to a lectureship in English at the University of Sydney, which made the Kiernans pioneers in what later became a minor exodus – the Careys, Williamsons, Oakleys and a number of others leaving Melbourne for sybaritic Sydney.

Just when I thought I was getting on top of sleepless teaching and settling into a routine, the principal called me into his office. He was a grave, authoritative man, and he asked me, gravely, authoritatively, whether I'd consider being sports master. The more I thought of it the more awful it sounded – so, true to my philosophy of constant movement to avoid responsibility, I applied for a vacancy in the Humanities Department of the Royal Melbourne Institute of Technology.

The interview was a frightening experience. I was confronted by a semi-circle of men, but I had my words ready. 'Inchoate' had got me into the university, and I had a small lexicon of others at hand: 'captious' – as in 'I don't want to sound captious, but in some ways Caulfield Technical College wasn't challenging enough.' 'Peremptory' also came in handy, as did 'lucubration', trotted out to let them know I studied at night; 'recondite' did not go amiss, and 'plethora' and 'hermeneutics' were also deployed. I thought afterwards I'd given them persuasive evidence that I would not teach English expression well, but I got the job.

I joined an institution that had neither bike racks (as in Mildura) nor sports, and was elevated to lecturer, but my stay was short. Long words had got me into the place, and five short ones got me out of it: STUDENT DRINKS BEER IN CLASS. These words were on a Melbourne *Herald* poster outside Flinders Street station as I, with hundreds of other gaberdined commuters, hurried under the clocks to catch a train home.

The student's name was Ryan, and the lecturer involved was me. I walked into the classroom on a Monday morning and Ryan (I later testified in court) was drinking beer from a bottle. He held it high, proudly, like a trumpeter doing a solo. I escorted him from the room and remonstrated with him (the perfect, formal courtroom word, as I continued with my evidence) in the corridor. The defendant (there he was, in the dock, tall, raw-boned, aged about twenty, with a sullen stare) then swore at me and threw a punch. It came at me slowly, and got no further than a shoulder. I grappled with him (another good courtroom word). To continue, in non-legal language: he lunged at me and ripped my shirt. I got him in a headlock, a hold I'd perfected from years of wrestles with my younger brother, and by the time we stopped I was ahead on points.

Ryan was found guilty of assault, and did a night in the slammer. (Later, tragically, he followed a girl to Tasmania, and when she rejected him he shot himself.) The head of the Humanities Department, an owlish bureaucrat, wasn't happy with the publicity. I told him he seemed more concerned about the press report than the welfare of his staff. Perhaps, he replied, it might be best if I left. I agreed with him, and went into advertising.

Has he come good yet?

In the employment ads, which I scanned regularly, I'd always been attracted to the sound of advertising copywriter, and decided now was the time to try to be one, despite the remonstrances of my father, ever ready to draw on his inexhaustible store of apothegms. ('Never give up a steady job.') He reminded me, unnecessarily, that I had a wife and four children to support, and this was not the time to jump ship (his phrase).

It was 1963 when I leapt from the railings. I was thirty-two, with a handful of stories published in magazines advertising people had never heard of. I was hired as a copywriter by the manager of an agency called National Advertising Services at £2500 a year (heady money for an ex-teacher). The manager, a charming man called Ron Walker, who looked like a more dignified version of Groucho Marx, was just back from Madison Avenue with a new way of writing ads that he'd learned from a hot agency called Doyle Dane Bernbach.

DDB (as those in the know called them) had developed a style so understated and clever the customer didn't think he was being sold a thing. In the middle of the shouting bazaar of the print ads was this silence, this sharp little half-tone. Picture: a Volkswagen. Caption: GET THE BUG. Copy: No frills. No fins. Just function.' And so on. Short sentences. Verbs? Forget 'em. Surbordinate clauses? Don't make me laugh. The art of the deafening whisper.

NAS had offices in smart St Kilda Road, and I exchanged a chalk-and-talk sports jacket for a new disguise: a sharp suit of hound's-tooth tweed. I was put in an office overlooking Melbourne Grammar with someone else Ron had gambled on: Morris Lurie. On my first morning, supersmart Barbara Robertson, who looked after the fashion side of the business, came in with a box of lingerie. She held up the unmentionables in turn – bras, panties, negligees – and said she needed something chic about each of them for a fashion brochure – and SAP.

'SAP?' I said, turning to Lurie who, in his navy-blue suit, looked as short and sharp as a DDB sentence.

'Soon as possible,' said Lurie. 'How long have you been in the business?'

'About forty minutes.' While I was lifting up the erotic underwear and gazing at them nonplussed, Lurie was already tapping at his typewriter, and in half an hour he'd done the lot.

Academic, prolix and bewildered, I was demoted to less demanding assignments. Paint-tin instructions for Dulux, VW dealer ads, copy for *Floor Cleaning Monthly*, *Quarry Mine and Pit*, and *Hardware Retailer*. For weeks I listened to exchanges I only half understood: letterpress, swing tickets, reverse type, fifty per-cent stipples, wet flongs, logo, repro and litho (wasn't he an Italian acrobat?).

The job tickets with copy requirements were brought into us by a begoggled and grinning office boy who knew a lot more about the business than I did. Ron Walker also thought Peter Carey might have possibilities, and when he wrote some Arabian-Nights copy about a new brand of perfume, he too joined the copy department, which was now moved to a flat further down St Kilda Road. Ron, who disliked the front-office meet-the-client charade, came with us. He was our copy chief, with a little office off our big one.

Lurie's Talmud, his guide to everything, was the *New Yorker*. He wore button-down Brooks Brothers shirts and cloth ties and bought Miles Davis records and read John Cheever stories, and while he dreamed of seeing his own fiction between the ads for whisky and pigskin luggage, he worked, as Carey and I did, on prose poems for shampoo and furniture and vinyl tiles, while Ron Walker turned out more copy than the three of us put together.

One day he opened the door to tell us Dunlop was launching a new range of golf clubs carrying Arnold Palmer's signature. Did we have any ideas? In half an hour he was back again, before we'd finished our morning coffee and jokes, with a piece of paper in his hand. 'When You're The King of Golf", he read to us, 'You don't sign anything new until it's perfect.' We applauded. Ron Walker was the king of copy.

Lurie and Carey were getting better and better, while I didn't seem to be improving at all. 'Ron's waiting for you to come good,' Lurie would tell me. Was he Ron's messenger or just being malicious? Probably both. Still, there was always the literary samizdat *Southerly* for an occasional story – and for Lurie, the *New Yorker* for the occasional rejection slip, often written in glowing terms. And then it was Peter Carey's turn. Tired of being the ninety-pound weakling on Literature Beach, he decided to have a go himself.

He called his novel *Wog*, and it was about a man who buries himself in a bunker. He showed us the opening chapter. It was unusual, not to say eccentric. 'Keep going,' I said. 'Don't bother,' added Lurie. 'Wasting your time.'

Carey did keep going, and just as Lurie encouragingly predicted, no one would publish it. But he was reading and learning fast. At the time, Carmel and I were battling it out in our cold-water weatherboard in Carnegie. We had no TV, no stereo, no car, and four little kids. Peter used to pick me up on a nearby corner on his way to work, and I paid him by giving him the books I reviewed for the *Sunday Australian*, which formed the basis for his literary education.

Unlike Lurie, I've always been an encourager – so I arranged for Carey and Leigh, his then partner, to meet the publisher John Hooker and his wife at dinner at our place. By that time, Hooker would have read the novel and be in a position to offer some comments. When suitably lubricated, he offered only one: 'I've read your manuscript, and my advice to you is that you're not a bad writer – you're not a writer at all.' Carey and Leigh, indignant, then left, leaving Carmel and me to put up with Hooker's fulminations. Later, when in bed, we were awakened by a phone call. It was Carey: 'I want that bastard's address.'

'Why?'

'So I can throw a brick through his window.' I thought it wise not to give it to him, but it didn't matter. Later, as Carey became more and more successful, metaphorical bricks went hurtling into the Hooker house, each heavier than the last.

On top of the world

Ron Walker waited eighteen months for me to come good. Then I gave notice and joined a bigger and duller agency – George Patterson's, where the account executives and their clients were harder nosed and snappy captions regarded as fancy. The hardest of the noses were attached to the flinty faces of Holden advertising managers. 'Don't give us clever,' they'd say. 'Give us punchy.'

The agency regarded their copywriters as tradesmen, to be tucked away at the end of a long corridor in a windowless attic out of sight of their clients. In this merciful isolation I joined Geoff Taylor, novelist and ex-bomber pilot. Our attic was directly above the Regent Theatre in Collins Street, and the soundtrack from afternoon movies would often beguile us as we toiled over our prose.

Because of its remoteness, our office attracted agency malcontents, who'd come up to have a smoke, tell a dirty story or, once it emerged that I was a Catholic father of four, spread *Playboy* centrefolds on my desk.

The Holden executives thought, rightly, that we were also remote from automotive reality, and one day we were taken on a tour of the factory at Fisherman's Bend. It was an experience

I've never forgotten. We paused at a door to be given protective glasses, and entered a roaring vastness, a jungle of pipes and cables. Liver-red engines floating high on circuits, intricate organisms waiting to be born. And beside us the assembly line begins, rising from the floor like a secret spring, taking the vehicles' bones on the long, slow road to completion.

Men go hard at it from every angle, screwing, riveting, hammering. They have time only to spare us a glance, lest the car inches out of their reach. Then the spray tents, then the drying ovens. Above us the engines dip and dive slowly down to be winched into the chassis. Conception: a Holden is formed. We were peering into capitalism's intricate guts, the intestinal line where the machines were created – that we, the admen in our pressed suits, had to polish into product. I felt guilty. We were the ones with the dirty hands.

Coming good was not hard at George Patterson's – there was no good to come to, just hard-selling copy. My main task was to write material for a magazine called *The Accelerator*, which promoted Holden spare parts to dealers under the NASCO brand. It was tedious work for both Geoff Taylor and me, and it was in reaction to this that a satirical home movie was planned.

Geoff brought in his old bomber-pilot helmet and leather jacket, Ridgway of the TV department provided a video camera, and Ramsay of radio did the lights and sound. At Ridgway's shout of Action!, Taylor, goggled, helmeted and Hitler-moustached, began a lunatic German gibbering in front of a map of Europe. At that moment, Dick Cudlipp, the general manager, came in to introduce a new member of staff. There was a brief freeze-frame, after which no possible explanation could be offered. 'I see,' said Cudlipp, and he did see. There was no foreman material here.

It was job-ad time again. There was one for an advertising copywriter in what looked like a safe haven – the Department of Overseas Trade. I collected my sad little advertising samples and presented them to the head of the Publicity Branch, a lean, mean and unsmiling man called A.C. Forrest. He flicked through my proofs without enthusiasm, then said he noted in my application that I'd published stories in magazines he'd never heard of. I explained that they were literary magazines. The word 'literary' seemed to set him off. 'You can forget about all that if you join us.' True to one of my maxims – agree with whatever is demanded of you and then ignore it – I replied, 'Of course.'

Always cover yourself

I got the job, and joined the confraternity of the public service. Trade Publicity was a journalists' graveyard where publications of varying degrees of dullness about Australian export products were produced. But I was the only copywriter, so I could set my own pace.

I wrote prose-poems about carpet sweepers, potato peelers, Nomad aircraft, swizzle sticks, eucalyptus-scented lavatory deodorants, dried fruits ('Australian dried fruits contain 15% more lactose and fructose than dried fruits from other countries'). If Australia exported it (or hoped to) I wrote copy for it: radio commercials for canned fruit in Swahili, ads in Japanese papers for toy koalas with pouch transistors that played 'Waltzing Matilda', passionfruit cordial in America, stainless-steel urinals in Peru.

This, I thought, might be the job I've always wanted – no competition, very little pressure, steady, undemanding employment with little chance of the sack, working away quietly amidst verities that seemed to be timeless.

First, The Power of Numbers. Everyone is graded mathematically. I was a Class 8 – a reasonably senior position in the Third Division which entitled you to a small office, with glass partitions (up to shoulder height only for Class 8s) and a rug underfoot – but not a carpet. Wall-to-wall came only with Class 10. You looked down on a 7, and up to a 9.

An 8 didn't have to sign the ordinary common time book but a more private one (where slightly more liberties could be taken). Class 9 and above didn't have to sign at all, but had to keep a diary of their arrivals and departures. As long as it was on record. As long as there was a piece of paper.

I was often late, and the personnel officer didn't like it. A meeting was called, and the complaint made. I explained that we now had five children and the mornings were difficult. The personnel officer, small, bald and fierce, was by now red in the face and banged the table: 'It's not just that you're late, it's the way you loiter! I've seen you! You saunter!'

The officer, whose name was Dance, bore another grudge. In our section, all desks faced inward to the corridor, except mine. The irregularity infuriated him, but he couldn't find anything in the regulations to make me turn my back to the window – it was a feeble protest, a stand for individuality. Turn my desk around and I'd slot into the bureaucratic machinery with a final deathly click.

Second, The File is Everything, and Everything is the File. As the body is made up of cells, so the bureaucracy is made up of files. Files swell, reproduce and spawn others. Files were stored in the hanging garden of the Registry. One must never hoard them or take them home. Bureaucratic battles take place within them. The important thing is to Cover Yourself. Once I neglected to do this and left a flank exposed. An aide-memoire later appeared in the file that was sharply critical of me, signed by a man who always seemed friendly. I sought an explanation from the Office Sage as to why the man hadn't broached it with me personally. There is file life, said the wise one, and real life, and they need have no connection whatever.

Positions Must be Filled. It was decided that an export action advertising campaign be discontinued, and the journalist responsible for it resigned, because there was nothing left for him to do. But his position still existed, and applications were invited, and a replacement found.

For a while, before I had my own office, I shared one with the new appointee. It took him a couple of days to realise there was nothing for him to do either. After a brief period of incredulity, he adjusted. He would open a file, lean back in his chair, rest the file on his chest and fall asleep, often with his mouth open. Filing clerks would sometimes use it as an in-tray to wake him up.

How could this be? I asked the Sage. Simple, he replied. If the position isn't filled, it will be abolished and disappear forever.

Myth of the Smiling Minister. Mr McEwen was Minister for Trade at the time, and there was a photo of him, friendly and smiling, on the receptionist's desk. One of my fellow Class 8s, deluded by this, decided one Friday on a bold course of action. Needing the minister's signature on an urgent document, and knowing that he was paying one of his visits to his Melbourne office, he decided to take the paper directly to him, rather than go through the slow-moving bureaucratic hierarchy.

So he walked down the rarely visited ministerial end of the corridor and braved his Cerberus of a secretary, who agreed, reluctantly, to get the sacred signature for him. He came back in triumph, little knowing what tremors he had set off.

The minister, furious that a flunkey had shown such temerity, complained to the Secretary of the Department, who passed the censure to the Deputy Secretary, who passed it on to a First Assistant Secretary, and then on down to the Assistant Secretary of the Publicity Branch, the lean and mean Mr Forrest, who dressed down the Deputy Director, who told my colleague that such a thing had never happened before and, if he valued his job, must never happen again. The public service might now have computers, but its structure, I'm sure, still goes back to the days of Byzantium.

Public service days tended to be dull. I divided them into quarters, with morning and afternoon tea and a lunchtime walk in Fawkner Park in between. Sometimes my boss and I were taken to lunch by design studios that wanted our advertising business. Since there's nowhere to hide in the modern office, I'd recuperate in the toilet, leaning uncomfortably against the flush handle, which pressed into my back. About three o'clock, if I were still recuperating, I'd hear the foot-dragging limp of an elderly alcoholic journalist who'd make himself comfortable in another cubicle – then there'd be the pop of the cork of his whisky flask.

Worse: one of the Australian trade commissioners working in the United States came in over a long weekend, entered a cubicle, took off his belt, looped it over the railing above the door, got up on the seat, and jumped. A day later, the caretaker saw his suspended feet in the gap under the door. He had done quickly what was happening to some of us in slow motion.

Under the pitiless fluorescence, layered in the files, powdered in the corners of desk drawers with the elastic bands and paper clips, lingered bureaucratic death, finer than dust.

Head down at night

I might have been coasting a little at work, but there was no chance of that at home. In 1966 Eugene, our fifth, had arrived, and every morning, as I took the St Kilda Road tram, I was escaping from work rather than going to it – but Carmel, the most efficient person I've known, managed superbly – so much so that I was able to write at night, once we'd got the quintet to sleep.

With two-and-a-half unpublished and unpublishable novels behind me, I turned to drama. My first effort was a one-acter about, predictably, a misfit trapped in the Public Service. It was called *Eugene Flockhart's Desk*, with the protagonist a research officer whose lifelong investigation of the poultry industry has led to uncontrollable outbreaks of arm-flapping and chook noises.

My theatrical effort got a single line in Peter Holloway's *Contemporary Australian Drama*: 'A reading of Oakley's first play in 1966 was the last theatrical performance at the Emerald Hill Theatre in Melbourne.' Hidden in this innocuous sentence are the kinds of embarrassments that, I'd later learn, seem to go with the nature of theatre itself.

The Emerald Hill Theatre had kept Melbourne dramatically nourished for five years. Its driving forces were Wal Cherry and George Whaley who mixed Sophocles and Ionesco with original Australian work, beginning with Bill Hannan's *Not With Yours Truly*, whose innovations included a dog on stage. Emerald Hill received insultingly modest funding from the Elizabethan Theatre Trust and worked in a climate that banned the newspaper advertising of one of its productions – *You'll Come to Love your Sperm Test*, directed by George Whaley. The theatre mocked the censorship by changing the title to *You'll Come to Love your Whale Test*, directed by George Spermley.

The *Flockhart* one-acter appeared with Tony Morphett's *I've Come About the Assassination*. Friends and relatives were summoned. Some of the latter thought they were going to The Theatre and dressed up instead of down. I did too, with my Department of Trade blue suit laughably incongruous amidst the rollneck sweaters of the Morphett camp.

Never mind. Interval's now over and here we are assembling for *Eugene Flockhart's Desk*, our formalities mercifully concealed as the house lights go down. The actors, who seem to have been costumed out of St Vincent de Paul bins, take their seats, consult their scripts, breathe in and begin – and, right on cue, a downpour thundered onto the tin roof. The actors' lips moved, but no words seemed to come out of them. The first half of the play disappeared, and the theatre itself soon followed.

Undeterred, I wrote another play, about another tormented figure, a teacher called Mr Stone. It was called *A Lesson in English*, and in it Stone tries to take his pubescent class through Marvell's *To His Coy Mistress*. The literary niceties are soon lost as the poem unleashes their primal urges, which take over the room.

It took the fancy of William Bates, who ran the modestly titled William Bates Theatre. Once again, family and friends were invited, and we trooped up the stairs to a small draughty space over a Carlton garage.

What awaited me was a humiliation rivalling that of Stone himself. Bates played the part of Stone, but didn't know his lines, and there were frequent whisperings from the wings. The ensemble work of the class he was meant to be instructing suggested they'd been brought in at random from the street. The chill wind that cut across the audience's legs was as nothing compared to the frigid spectacle on the stage. I spent most of the time with my head down, waiting for the anarchy to finish.

After the charade I was led, a condemned man, to an area divided off by a torn emerald drape. The green room. Sherries were served by a man in a dinner suit. I was asked to speak, but would not. Two old ladies who had come all the way from Ballarat asked me to sign their programs. I stumbled down the stairs afterwards vowing never to write another play.

I sank back into prose, and wrote another novel. It was called *A Wild Ass of a Man*, and it bore the marks of desperation. It tried to be one continuous breathless passage. It was hectic and sometimes overwritten, with occasional colouring from J.P. Donleavy's *The Ginger Man*.

It traced the progress of yet another comically doomed figure called Muldoon – his Catholic boyhood, his foolish undergraduate days, his disasters with teaching, advertising and girls. Finally, rejected by everybody, Muldoon is seized by a desire to announce that the end of the world is at hand, and suffers a revolving crucifixion on a Luna Park ferris wheel.

It did the usual rejection rounds, gently decaying each time, until John Hooker of Cheshires took pity on the tattered state of the manuscript and took it in. I was so grateful I accepted the meagre advance, submitted to his editing and made no objection to the frantic design of the jacket. Would there be any publicity? I timidly asked. 'Ah,' said Hooker. 'Come with me.'

He led me to a room behind Cheshire's bookshop and showed me a piece of white cardboard with the name of the novel and its author hand-lettered on it, which would be 'prominently displayed' – his words – in the adjoining bookshop. 'There's your publicity,' he said, apparently without irony.

And so it was released – almost furtively, like a petty criminal from prison. There were isolated handclaps here and there; the Catholic Advocate declared it unsuitable for school libraries, and the venerable A.R. Chisholm remarked on 'the torrential character of the writing, which is feverish but strangely controlled'. Despite a leg-up from Brian Kiernan – 'Funniest since Furphy' – it didn't sell well. The most significant thing about *A Wild Ass of a Man* was that it led Cheshires to abandon publishing fiction. In a year, I had closed a theatre and amputated a leading publisher's fiction arm.

Mama mia

Given my developing record, it was surprising to be invited to a meeting arranged by the formidable artistic matriarch Betty Burstall early in 1967 at what was to become one of the centres of Melbourne radicalism – the Hannans' terrace in North Melbourne. Bill and Lorna Hannan had already plotted a breakfast revolution – they were the first to my knowledge to introduce muesli, holding up packs of what appeared to be birdseed to their bemused friends – and were later to attempt bold experiments in education (Sydney Road Community School, where the students had a big say in what was studied and how the school ran) and family life (a group of households forming an economic union, sharing their incomes and just about everything else).

As we sat around in a semicircle on a Sunday morning, Betty enthused about a new kind of theatre she'd seen in New York – not a place of foyers and curtains and audiences sitting cut off in the dark, but performances in off-off-Broadway cafés where new kinds of plays were being produced – no props, no make-up: a direct, hard-hitting theatre with the actors right there in front of you, close enough to touch.

Betty, who managed to be regal and alternative at the same time, had it all worked out. The idea would be transplanted here, and she'd found the place for it – a disused underwear factory in Faraday Street Carlton. She was going to rent the shabby old building (for twenty-eight dollars a week), put in tables and chairs, serve coffee, and – looking around at us – put on some plays.

She called it La Mama – after the pioneering New York space of the same name – and it opened with Jack Hibberd's *Three Old Friends*. This was followed by my *Witzenhausen Where Are You?* – about a messenger in a big corporation who locks himself in the toilet and issues apocalyptic notes under the door.

My third play there – *It's A Chocolate World* – was performed in stifling summer heat (La Mama was a sweatbox). Peter Cummins, as the managing director of a chocolate factory, had to wear a suit. At every pause in the action, as sweat poured off him, he glared at me, unwisely in the front row no more than a couple of metres away. At the end, as the dutiful applause faded and everybody rushed for the exit and fresh air, Peter tore his jacket off and gave me an unscripted line – 'I'm going to be the first managing director in a fucking singlet.'

The realistic La Mama style had its drawbacks. When

the actor/director Peter Carmody was performing there, the woman he was on stage with threw a fit and collapsed writhing to the floor. 'This woman's in trouble,' he said, 'she needs help.' There was an admiring pause from the audience – this was the kind of acting they'd come to see. 'Look!' he shouted. 'No jokes. This woman is ill!' Wonderful. Alternative theatre at its best. 'She's having a fit, you fools!' he roared, as he ran out into the street for help.

La Mama gained strength and standing as playwrights – Hibberd, Romeril, Williamson, Buzo and many others – saw their plays evolve in workshops, and everything that was vital in local theatre seemed to crystallise around it. Not only plays, but poetry, music, dance – the night's program was chalked on a blackboard by the door, and the Carlton population of students, academics, bohemians and boozers filled the place every night (it only needed 60 to do it).

Max Chapman, a faithful audience member since the beginning, put the experience thus: 'I have been interrogated under arc lights, lowered blindfolded through a trapdoor, abused by actors, drunk gallons of coffee and met great people. Frozen in winter, boiled in summer. I have been bored beyond endurance, witnessed an actor defecate on stage, then, just as despair began to engulf me, a brilliant play emerges.'

Tigerland

Like Betty Burstall, my wife is a driving force, and she decided it was time we left our characterless house in Carnegie – especially as we now had five children. The inner suburbs were

Uh-oh: pregnant again.

calling, and early in 1969 the call was answered, and the caravanserai moved to Richmond.

We were pioneer gentrifiers of the area, bringing claret and corduroy into beer-drinking territory. Francis Street was narrow, and lined with tightly packed single-fronted cottages. Our house was double-fronted, with courtyard and outbuildings – a manor by comparison. It had been passed in at $11,500, and our offer later of $12,000 was accepted.

'Mad,' said my estate agent father, falling back on his rich repertoire of maxims. 'When you buy, you move up, not down.' He called Richmond a 'dirty, filthy place'. (He'd not long been back from a tour of Europe, where he'd also found Italy and Greece to be dirty, filthy places.) He said these things walking up and down the potholed footpath in front of our fence. 'We're going to convert the outbuildings into bedrooms for the five kids. They'll be across the courtyard, where they can make a bit of noise. There's a huge living room, a modern kitchen, and it's cheap.'

I had to explain all this to him because he refused to set foot in the place. 'It's cheap because no one in their right mind would buy it. You'll never get your money back.' Then he got into his yellow Holden and drove off. We lived in the house for seven years. A sixth child later arrived, but my father never did. Then we sold it, considerably renovated, for $44,000, which I delighted in telling my father. (I didn't tell him that as soon as the new owners moved in, the fleas that had been dormant all winter rose up out of the seagrass matting and attacked them en masse. We paid for the fumigation.)

Not long after we'd moved in, Carmel, weakened by flu, stress and the labour of interior painting, caught hepatitis and turned the colour of sulphur. The doctor said she should go to Fairfield Infectious Diseases Hospital, but she would not. So everyone else in the family had to have a gamma globulin shot. 'It's a pretty solid injection,' the doctor whispered, 'you go first to show them there's nothing to it.'

'There's nothing to it, see?' he said to them. 'Look at Dad.' As I lay on my stomach with my pants around my knees I saw him advancing on me with what looked like Don Quixote's lance, which he sank into my right cheek. It hurt, but I tried not to show it. The kids weren't fooled, and scattered. I got up and went after a couple, limping stiffly across the courtyard. The two girls had disappeared into the back lanes of Richmond, but I got one boy down from the garage roof by his ankle. A second leapt at the back fence like a demented kangaroo, and the third hid in his tree house, drawing the rope ladder after him. 'Be a man,' I said to him. 'But I'm not a man, I'm a boy.' The boy later became a philosopher.

Even in 1969 Richmond was rich in ethnicities. Bridge Road was a roaring thoroughfare of nationalities, as if the Mediterranean had been laid out in a straight line. Commonplace now, exotic then: cevapi, fetta, baklava, mozzarella and, moving up and down the footpath, an old man selling fresh Greek bread from his trolley, with propellers on sticks for the kids. On a windy day his airscrews spun so fast I imagined him taking off and floating over the suburb, Chagall-style.

Sleepless in Richmond (the printery at rear went day and night).

As our first Richmond Christmas approached, Bridge Road's pulse beat even harder, and Southern European emotions became even more intense. Tribal hostilities were somehow involved with the local fish and chip shop, and late one Sunday afternoon it exploded in a roar of flake and potatoes. A couple of days before two large Sicilian women had had a tremendous brawl outside the greengrocer's, with one whirling the other by the hair and scattering her vegetables across the footpath.

Things were heating up. One December morning Jimmy, who lived on the corner, appeared at the front door in his dark blue railwayman's uniform with Watchman on the cap to tell me he'd put a bullet through the next kid who let his tyres down. Fortunately, he was little, but the man from across the road was not. He'd come red-faced and roaring out of his house and tell the kids in the street he worked night shift and they'd better shut up or else. The kids would scatter, shouting Greek and Italian obscenities, and then he'd charge over to me and we'd have a shouting match. Next time, he bellowed, he'd have a go at me.

On Christmas Eve we decided to do it the European way, and give the kids their presents that night. Instead of ending his run at our place, Santa would start there, clicking the front gate. They were to stay in their rooms and not peep, until they heard the gate. When it got dark the presents were rapidly arranged around the tree like cane toads around a Queensland streetlight. Then I clicked.

The children rushed over, and the ripping and tearing began. There was some muttering about the paucity of presents, but we had a surprise. On the morning itself, corrugated-iron panels were brought out of hiding and assembled into a crude circle, which was then filled with water and shrieking children. In the congestion one of the panels gave way, and a great wave gushed down the drive and across the narrow street, where it headed for an old Greek lady in black. She broke into an awkward Hellenic canter, but was saved by the gutter, at which the water lapped.

Night shift, provoked by the noise, emerged, swinging fists the size of hams, shouting that we were going to settle this 'here and now'.

'You're right,' I said, and held out my hand and wished him a happy Christmas. Abashed, he enveloped it in his and invited me in for a beer. Richmond had accepted us.

Disgusting passages

On 6 July 1970, twenty guests sat down to a lunch arranged by Dennis Wren of Heinemanns to celebrate the publication of my second novel, *A Salute to the Great McCarthy*, the story of (I quote from the blurb) ' a brilliant young footballer from the bush determined to make good in the bright lights of the city'. He does, briefly, then (blurb again) 'women, football, coaches and businessmen all get him down in the end'.

I was heavy with influenza, about to become a father (my wife dared not attend) for the sixth time, and in a state of terror at having to address the gathering, which included such seventies media luminaries as Gerald Lyons, John Larkin, Andrew McKay and Elizabeth Auld, with a ballasting of literati (Ian Turner and Stephen Murray-Smith). But wait – one invitee was missing. We waited, and then he walked in – John Coleman, the greatest full-forward ever to play the game – apart, maybe, from Bob Pratt, whom I was too young to see.

Coleman had retired in 1954 when still in his prime (he'd damaged his knee after one of his sensational leaps). He was still trim and fit and handsome, though deathly pale (he would die of a heart attack three years later). Attention and questions gradually turned from the nervous novelist to him. Who wants to hear someone who only imagined playing football when you can talk to the real thing? He told me he'd enjoyed the book (a footballer who's read a book!), especially the part about McCarthy's first game as a full-forward. 'You got it exactly,' he said. Aided in no small measure by a brief appearance in that position with the West St Kilda Catholic Young Men's Society.

So the book was launched, followed one week later by Kieran, our sixth (and last). I too was having an obstetric experience, moving from uterine obscurity to the wider world. There were interviews and enthusiastic reviews, and as a result the novel sold well, and stayed in print for twenty-five years.

And then there were six.

It appeared on school syllabus lists, where it gained, at least in the West, notoriety: FOL FIGHTS SCHOOL FILTH ran the headline. 'A deputation has presented a petition of more than 5,500 signatures to the WA Premier, Sir Charles Court, demanding that "filthy, indecent or blasphemous words and incidents or excessive violence be exised (sic) from books read in English classes – including *Catch 22*, *The Chant of Jimmy Blacksmith* and *A Salute to the Great McCarthy*". FOL (Festival of Light) chairman Mr Ray Ellery claimed the disgusting passages in these books were upsetting thousands of the State's parents and children. He called for the Superintendent of English, Mr Peter Gunning, to be suspended.' An author couldn't have wished for more.

Becomes Freemason

Thus encouraged, we bought our first car, a second-hand Holden station wagon, and Carmel learned to drive it. A mother of five, and now a nursing mother of a sixth for merely two months, and she learns to drive? She had long ago resigned herself to the fact that she was saddled with not simply a non-driver but someone with a practical incapacity that bordered on the pathological. (My father had tried to teach me in his pre-war Plymouth, but the hand-and-foot co-ordination involved in double-declutching between second and third gear was beyond me.)

It wasn't easy to back the big Holden into the drive, so I'd stand by the gate and help with directions. Neighbouring men would nod understandingly, thinking I was giving Mum driving lessons. 'They never learn, do they?' offered one, and I could only nod in rueful agreement.

The pantechnicon more or less mastered, it was soon used to ferry supplies for a party to celebrate the winning of the Captain Cook Bicentenary Award for fiction (jointly with Tom Keneally) for *Let's Hear it for Prendergast*, my third novel. A piano was trundled in, as was the pianist, Dick Hughes, who played Dixieland jazz for the hundred guests, while Kieran, at four-and-a-half months, tried to make sense of it all from his pram, while inhaling fumes of tobacco and alcohol with subtle undertones of hash. It was a prodigious feat of catering and cooking, and Carmel, with me as witless kitchen hand, did it all. One guest, the editor of a Melbourne literary magazine, showed his appreciation by getting drunk and pissing in a corner of one of the children's bedrooms.

To get the as-yet unpublished novel out as rapidly as possible, a Heinemanns editor had been dispatched to Adelaide to check the proofs, but alcohol may have affected him too. I counted seventy typos in the rushed-out edition. But the reviewers didn't seem to notice. 'Ferociously funny,' said the very elderly A.R. Chisholm in the *Age*. Even the unsmiling Scot John Douglas Pringle lapsed into an untypical Australian metaphor in the *Sydney Morning Herald*: 'Australia's greatest humorist – by a furlong.' (Now the word is meaningless.)

The gestation of *Let's Hear it for Prendergast* involved so much drinking that it was no wonder the novel was brought to birth impaired. Dennis Wren insisted on lunch whenever a matter had to be discussed, which entailed the consumption of alcohol until nightfall. He was an enthusiast and visionary, who moved his company into spacious new offices in St Kilda. His own office was on this ample scale, with ensuite bathroom and revolving bookcase that opened onto a bar. His extravagance later proved his downfall. The managing director of Heinemanns made a special trip out from London to sack him. 'I want you out of the building (but it was Dennis's building!) today,' the urbane assassin was alleged to have said. I imagined him sitting on a box of books on the footpath, wondering what had happened, and where he'd go for lunch.

The early seventies were heady times in publishing. Penguin Books, not to be outdone, opened even larger premises in Ringwood, a Melbourne outer suburb, where, at the launch party, I was required to operate a Heath Robinsonian publishing machine created by Bruce Petty. It involved the flicking of switches and turning of wheels. The intricate innards would spin and hum, and a book would drop out at the end.

Guests then went out to a courtyard and got down to business. One of the most distinguished, a poet and academic, did his not infrequent falling-down number, and had to be dragged to the sidelines. Was there a doctor in the house? There was. The pioneer playwright Jack Hibberd diffidently gave him mouth-to-mouth, while drinking went on uninterrupted.

By now, after six children, what the Catholic Church – picking up the phrase with surgical gloves – called artificial methods of birth control, were now essential. What was pronounced evil by the Church was a blessing for us, so we joined the exodus and left.

Too embarrassed to ask for condoms over the counter, we got them mail-order and stowed them under the mattress. They were found by one of our young sons. My mother was visiting at the time, and our son ran out of our bedroom blowing into a slowly inflating sausage, yelling, 'Balloons! Hidden balloons!'

After leaving the Church, I was welcomed into the

freemasonry of drink, in which publishing occupied one of the most active lodges. John Hooker, the publisher of my first novel, took his masonic duties extremely seriously, the password being lunch or dinner. We were dining with him and his wife (both now dead) one evening at a table forested with bottles, when he became incandescent, and turned on each guest, prefacing each insult with 'and as for you . . .' Finally, he reached his wife. 'And as for you,' he said, 'unlike the others, you are not second rate. You are third rate.' She ran crying upstairs to the bedroom, with the host hurrying after her to apologise. Then he called down to us from the landing: 'Just talk amongst yourselves.'

Hooker left Cheshires for Penguin Books, which, with assistance from the managing director, he turned into a dining club. As with Dennis Wren, business was always done at lunch. Hooker, along with many other publishing initiatives, decided to reprint my first novel as a Penguin paperback: lunch; and he would do the same with my second and third: lunches, usually until nightfall.

The seventies in Australia were the last bacchanalian decade. Jogging was rare, aerobics unheard of, smoking perfectly acceptable. But a stage was reached when the collective liver couldn't take it any more. Enjoyment lost its innocence. The few literati who survived into old age, their lungs blackened and noses veined, look back on that time with nostalgia. The bad times have been filtered out, leaving only rosy memories of couples drinking and arguing around a table, and perhaps doing some touching up under it. As a friend put it – 'Thank heavens we could only afford casks then – otherwise my first wife would have thrown bottles.'

The gap between the bricks

We were mobile now, and this made Christmas more complicated. Christmas Eve with presents and tree, then the day itself at my parents' place in East St Kilda, with still more presents. I can still see, in memory, the spectacle of us on our way: two adults, six children, pusher, pram, pudding, presents. Reflected in the Chapel Street shop windows, we looked very low in the water. What if we got a flat tyre? How will I reach the spare? Where do you put the jack? Was I the only man in Australia who couldn't change a tyre?

My mother's impeccable lounge, violated every Christmas.

My mother's been up since six preparing. My father's organised drinks, turkey, ham. The Springtime dinner set is out – white plates bordered with English garden yellows, greens and blues. My grandmother is helped up the front steps. Her cheeks are flushed, her makeup out of register, like bad colour printing. She's puffing and talking at the same time.

We begin in the lounge under the Rupert Bunny portrait of my mother. We exchange gifts. My grandmother's obsession with waste has reached the stage where she saves pieces of cardboard (to make into Christmas cards), newspapers to sell to the butcher, milk bottle tops and silver paper for Oxfam, bits of string. My father, affable over his beer, pats the children on the head: 'And which one are you?'

We move into the dining room and take up our positions. My grandmother, who seems to have starved herself for days, disposes of her serving and then has the children's leftovers. It's warming up. Faces are getting flushed. At a certain point, hoping to provoke me, my father will say something about the Catholic Church: the Pope's wealth, the tunnels between the convents and the presbyteries, the slave laundries.

Carmel's pudding is served from the auto tray so that my mother can turn her back and push five-cent pieces into each portion. We give ours to the kids, but my grandmother keeps hers, and delivers her annual homily on the importance of thrift. 'Look after the pennies,' she says, as if she's just made it up, 'and the pounds will look after themselves.'

At the end of the meal, my father goes to his bed and begins snoring immediately, as if stunned by a club. The carpet under the table is like a relief map. Cleaning up begins, and preparation for afternoon tea. My brother, his wife and their six children arrive, and more presents are unwrapped. My mother normally keeps the lounge room dusted and polished. Boxes, paper, plastic, toys, plates, food, noise – today its violation is total.

My brother and his family leave first. When he's gone, I get the key to the cellar to steal a couple of bottles of wine from the cases he keeps stored there. As I crouch down and go in,

I'm overpowered by a smell of dryness and dust, a tomb smell. Beyond the bottles there's a gap between the bricks. It leads to a gloomier gloom, a rat-and-spider place I was never as a child brave enough to go into.

Fear of the dark was still there, waiting. It's because of this primal fear that the light of the tree on the hearth means so much to kids, almost as much as the gifts around it. Perhaps for them Christmas is still a primitive festival, celebrating the year's turning, like a door opening and a light coming on.

Phantom hisser exposed

'The place should be shut down,' said the man from the Health Department, as he looked aghast at the moribund building which the La Mama Company was planning to move into. It was virtually a shell – but after weeks of painting, hammering, welding and wiring, the place that had once been a pram factory became the Pram Factory, with a three-year lease negotiated by the entrepreneurial John Timlin for one hundred dollars a week.

The La Mama practitioners now called themselves the Australian Performing Group, and with the bigger venue developed a more expansive style. For their first show, *Marvellous Melbourne* (December 1970), they went back to the melodramas of the 1880s – the last time there'd been a popular theatre.

Alfred Dampier's 1889 extravaganza of the same name was turned on its head, to reveal, in song, stereotype and swagger, the proud city's seething underside: the larrikins, the corrupt politicians, the opium dens and brothels. It was vital, visual, vaudevillian, and it was rough. Less-than-Marvellous Melbourne was re-worked, and when it reopened in March the following year was a hit.

Later that year came another – David Williamson's *Don's Party* – frowned on by some of the ideologues of what was now called the Collective because, as a piece of straightforward realism about the middle-class, it veered dangerously close to the despised repertoire of the Melbourne Theatre Company.

But they had it wrong. It's not a middle-class party. The characters are ocker and crude. Years later, when I saw a London production, with slack-jawed yobboness played to the hilt, to the delight of the English audience having their view of Australia confirmed, I wanted to run out of the theatre screaming, 'This isn't us!' Instead, I just ran out of the theatre.

Don's Party was followed by a third hit – *The Feet of Daniel Mannix* – about the immoveable, immemorial Archbishop of Melbourne, who'd been at the centre of nearly every national controversy for fifty years. Perhaps in revenge for what I'd had to endure for at least twenty of them, I made him a comic, vaudevillian figure. His fight against secular education was done as a tag wrestle; his clash with W.M. Hughes over conscription during World War I becomes a gun battle; his arrest by the English off the coast of Ireland is done in bathtubs.

Bruce Spence played the lofty, looming Mannix, and Max Gillies, in green tights and cloak, was the slightly sinister Greensleeves. Gillies had studied B.A. Santamaria's weekly TV show until he sounded more like the man than Santamaria himself. There were songs written by Williamson and John Romeril, music by Lorraine Milne and direction by Graeme Blundell.

Almost everyone liked it, except the Catholic Advocate

('mean and spiteful') and, one night, a phantom hisser. It was also a night when I was on front of house. The hisser's timing was flawless – vehement sibilance at every pause in the action. I tracked it down to an elderly man in horn-rimmed glasses whom I recognised as the author and journalist Cyril Pearl.

At the end, he counterpointed the applause with alliterative cries of bosh! bollocks! baloney! I was in charge of the lights on the exit steps, and when he tottered to the brink I turned them off, and he half-tumbled down to the dustbins.

Day to day, hour to hour

On 13 November 1971, when *Daniel Mannix* was packing them in at the Pram Factory, we were unable to do front of house because two of our children were sick with German measles and croup. To ease their crouping, we prepared an inhalation of creosote and boiling water. Kieran, now sixteen months, was at the reaching-and-pulling stage. He did exactly that with the plastic creosote container, and the boiling water went all over him. We took off his skivvy and the skin of his arm came off with it.

We rang our doctor, who told us to take him straight to the Children's Hospital. We put two other kids in the back, and while I held Kieran, writhing and screaming in a sheet, Carmel, who'd only recently learned to drive, ran red lights all the way to the hospital, where he was given a pain-killing injection and taken away.

Kieran had third-degree burns to thirty per cent of his body. Nineteen seventy-two was the hardest year of his life – and ours. He needed skin grafts, and when he came back from hospital his arm had to be kept straight in a pink plastic splint for a few hours each day. He couldn't play properly, but Carmel, a Mother Teresa of patience, played records of his favourite songs and danced with him to take his mind off his pain. He woke a lot at night. He was a full-time job, and we had five other small children as well.

Every Wednesday my mother came over, and Carmel went into town to do an adult education philosophy course. It was the only thing that kept her sane. The future didn't exist. There was only the present. Not good days and bad days but good hours and bad hours. But by 1973 it became a little easier for Kieran and for us. Thanks to Gough Whitlam, university fees were abolished, enabling Carmel to begin an arts course part-time. And also thanks to Gough Whitlam, I could help more: I got a literary grant.

The happy corner and the nasty corner

Back in the unreal world, the Pram Factory did another play of mine – *Beware of Imitations*. They'd had a good year, with Jack Hibberd's *Stretch of the Imagination*, the Hannans' *Compulsory Century* and Katherine Susannah Prichard's *Brumby Innes*. *Beware of Imitations* kept the good box-office times going.

I'd had to endure two benevolent dictators, and now that Mannix had been mocked it was time for the second: R.G. Menzies. I provided a script, and Bill Hannan (as director), Max Gillies (as Menzies) and Bruce Spence (as the suffering servant) did wonders with it. Max and Bruce got on as if in a dream – and their improvisational romance was creatively chaperoned by Bill Hannan. It was the most exciting improvising I'd ever been involved in, and made the Pram Factory's tenet about group direction seem right – but the reason wasn't so much the tenet as the talent.

In a nursing home, Sir Wilfred McLuckie dreams of the past and dictates his memoirs to his servant, with crucial episodes re-enacted, and a finale showing McLuckie's horror as he sees student demonstrators violating the Shrine of Remembrance. At the end, 'a giant earthworm with a wide loose mouth sucks him in – he's engorged, like a frog entering a snake'. (Thirty-seven years later, the symbolism of this escapes me.)

At the Pram Factory, opening nights were dramas in themselves. Anything could go wrong, and usually did. The play featured a Nasty Corner, with red flag and picture of Ben Chifley, and a Happy Corner, with Union Jack and portrait of the Queen. In Act One, Sir Wilfred performs an elaborate sycophantic dance, to music, sinking to his knees and finally his stomach in obeisance to the Queen. Gillies had developed an exotic mix of steps and swayings, but on opening night the music didn't come on, and he had to do it in silence.

I can still see the death-pale face of John Sumner, the director of the Melbourne Theatre Company, as he watched this heroic performance, grim-faced and unsmiling, while the audience roared and whistled all around him. The overall result, to quote *The Perambulator* (the Australian Performing Group's newsletter), was 'its biggest-ever box-office success – bigger even than *Don's Party*!'

Modest financial success made no difference to the take-it-or-leave-it facilities endured by the audience. Bare boards to sit on, bitter proletarian coffee in chipped mugs, third-world toilets: no middle class comforts here. Backstage could be just as demanding. I never felt comfortable at meetings of the Collective. In the eyes of many in this intimidating entity, the idea of individual talent was bourgeois and elitist – no stars, no power-wielding directors, and no self-styled writers either. Since you can't do plays simply by hating capitalism and all-in-it-together enthusiasm, the result was some total turkeys.

In their zeal to show the working classes what was good for them, the Group once took a play called *Money* to the canteen of the Rosella soup factory. It was a marriage of Marx and *Sesame Street*, simplistic and patronising, and the immiserated workers voted with their cutlery, which clacked on indifferently while the lecture-pantomime was being performed.

At one end of the Pram Factory building lived the Tower Children – a group within the Group, family-hating dopesters, communitarians, anarcho-surrealists, insurrectionary feminists, with matching headgear – Afghan knits, Harlem tea-cosies, cowboy hats, Cultural Revolution caps. Their heroes were the three Ms: Marx, Marcuse and Mao. In the words of Tim Robertson, in his effervescent history of the Pram Factory – 'The Great Helmsman was prominent among the household gods of the Tower. The bad news about the Cultural Revolution went unheard. The Red Guards were seen as a bit over the top, but basically okay.'

Robertson, in trying to catch the tone of those on the hard left, exaggerates only a little: 'In solidarity with the fucking working class, theatre was a fucking means not an end. A fucking weapon in the class war. A fucking waddy to fucking whack your fucking weltschmerz into the fucking weltanschauung that would lead to the dictatorship of the fucking proletariat, mate.'

As a Catholic father of six who'd worked in advertising, living in a tidy, even stylish house (get a look at this!) I sometimes felt I was the Enemy They Had to Have. I couldn't abide the fulminations of John Romeril and Lindzee Smith about capitalism (faulty yes, evil no). Romeril predicted that by 2000, capitalism would be dead. In the cruellest of ironies, by then the Pram Factory had been demolished and replaced by a shopping mall.

At the end of 1974 I submitted a play called *Bedfellows* to the Group, which voted that it go to the Programming Committee, to which I was summoned to make my pitch. The committee was dominated by a Gang of Two – Lindzee Smith, who could see nothing wrong with the terrorist bombing of innocent civilians if it furthered the revolution, and Jon Hawkes, a pony-tailed counter-cultural who was also an accountant (could one be both?).

I was treated to an hour's patronising interrogation about why I thought an institution as obsolete as marriage (and its even quainter concomitant, adultery) was worth writing about. I replied that the justification, if there were one, lay in the script. They'd found it diverting in an antiquated middle-class way. They let it through reluctantly, as if it were infected, and as I was dismissed there were whispers . . . 'crock o'shit'.

So *Bedfellows* was done at the beginning of 1975. Had I been paranoid, a feeling the Collective tended to inspire, I'd have wondered why my plays were always put on in high summer, when the theatre was stifling. Jack Hibberd directed, Max Gillies, Fay Mokotow and Bill Garner performed.

True to the APG's Opening Night Principle, something went wrong. The play opens with Paul, a middle-aged academic, dozing off in his chair. ('Enter Carol with milk bottles, which she clinks in his ear.') Fay clinked too hard and the bottles broke, covering the floor with broken glass. Fay was barefooted, and what followed was almost a formal dance, as she and Gillies zipped and zapped around the glass. The unhappily married couple and the play survived, and it became a hit, with people being turned away and an extended season, followed by a national tour.

The only one who didn't like it (apart from the Gang of Two) was Bill Garner, who played the part of Gillies's cuckolder. He told me he disliked it so much that he had to go to the Albion Hotel to anaesthetise himself before his appearance in Act Two. Garner, a member of the worker-control down-with-directors left, saved his best theatrical performances for Collective meetings. He acted best when not on stage.

My strangest friend

I had encouraged Peter Carey, only to have the dubious satisfaction of seeing him sail past me. I also encouraged Gerald Murnane, and it happened again. I remember nothing of our first meeting, but Gerald, who retains everything, describes it thus: 'One hot evening in late 1964, Catherine (his wife) and I visited you and your family in Carnegie. I still recall my feeling of mild embarrassment. I would have worn a sports jacket and tie. I suppose she wore a twin-set. We arrived at feeding time. I'm sure we got a glass of wine or a cup of coffee and a snack, but all I recall is child after child being served with a large bowl of ice cream and then carrying it round the room and eating it on the run, as it were. (Only a few years later, with three children in nappies, Catherine and I were organising our own feeding sessions).'

At some later stage Gerald showed me some of his work – handwritten pieces recounting, if I remember correctly, the daily confessions of a would-be writer, in response to which I was forced to use my Peter Carey word, 'unusual'. (Not to say eccentric, I thought to myself.) And again, as with Peter Carey, I urged him to keep going.

He did, and would have done so without any encouragement from me. Gerald's first novel, *Tamarisk Row*, appeared in 1974, and he held a dinner party in celebration. First, a photo album was passed around, containing a pictorial biography of the author. Later, the author blows a whistle, and we're told to change places with others. When I remarked on the magnified marble on the cover of the book, he told me it was one of those referred to in the childhood chapters, and then led me into a room of filing cabinets, where he pulled out a drawer, selected a file marked M, and produced the marble in question, preserved for all those years. Then we returned to the dining room, and he blew the whistle again.

Still in my role as encourager, I brought his third novel, *The Plains*, to the attention of the *Sydney Morning Herald*'s literary editor, who'd never heard of him. I gave it an enthusiastic review. It was published by an obscure press in a jacket that resembled a piece of grey serge, and I declared it to be 'like a diamond hidden in flannelette'. Gerald's response was a muted thanks. The best review, he pointed out, had appeared elsewhere, but he was grateful I had covered his 'exposed northern flank'.

We fell out when I was critical of *Inland*, his fourth novel. I wrote that I sometimes got lost in the circuitous sentences, forever coiling themselves around their subject – a writer watching himself write. A long epistolary silence followed. Much later, when I found out that Catherine was dying of cancer, our friendship revived, and he told me, in his monotonal matter-of-fact way, what she and he were enduring. When the disease advanced, Catherine couldn't sleep for more than an hour at a time, and thus neither could he, and this went on for a month before her death.

Some time after that, Gerald sent me an extraordinary document: Details of the Archives of Gerald Murnane. They consisted of: The Literary Archive, with photographs of the filing cabinets, opened and closed, which contained drafts of everything the author had ever written, letters to and from publishers and comments from reader and reviews; The Chronological Archive, seventeen drawers packed with files carrying such titles as How I Fell Out With Barry Dickins, Peter Goldsworthy, Helen Garner, Gerard Windsor, Rodney Hall (and me); 10,000 anagrams of Gerald Murnane; A Letter About My Bowel Movements et al; Judith Wright, Hypocrite and Liar; Objects that Wink at Me; 3000 Words About Naked Females; more than 1000 Illustrations of Naked Women Removed From Girlie Magazines and Marked With Coloured Stickers To Explain My Reasons For Preserving Them; and The Antipodean Archive – about 800 pages of manuscripts, maps, sketches describing the organisation of horse-racing in two imaginary countries, reporting in detail the results of hundreds of races run in each country.

In his accompanying letter Gerald said he'd welcome any comments, so I told him the material was both extraordinary and somewhat disturbing. To me the archives revealed (I summarise) a solipsistic belief that the self is the only reality – a self so documented that there's a sense of seeing himself endlessly repeated in mirror after mirror, for which the French have a phrase – mis dans l'abime (plunged into the abyss). Gerald was outraged – the other recipients – librarians – had nothing but praise. With Gerald, if you weren't an admirer you were an enemy, and now I was one.

'What have I done?'

I'd penetrated fictional and theatrical territory, but cinema remained unexplored. One day a plangent voice – 'This is David Baker phoning' – invited me into it. He had just read *The Great McCarthy*, he brayed, and found it 'highly risible'. He had directed TV series innumerable – the placement of the adjective was his – and now he thought it time to branch out. In short, he sang, a movie. Could this be discussed over a lunch? Disconcerted though I was by his manner, I replied that it could.

Carmel and I drove up to Warrandyte, then still sylvan and rural, where Baker welcomed us into a bush house built largely of wooden poles, and provided a lubricated lunch. Then he rose and started pacing the room. He was a big man, with good legs, which he showed off in short shorts and, liberated by chardonnay, began his pitch.

He'd read the novel three times, and it had retained its risibility throughout. There were many situations that would lend themselves to film, and he'd lined up a screenwriter codger – John Romeril, whom I knew well – who should fill the bill. Codger? Risibility? Was the novel safe with this man?

Baker then went to the end of the dining area to the toilet

door, and left it open as he unzipped. 'I know what you're thinking,' he brayed as he pissed, 'you are cogitating on one thing and one thing only: lucre.' The cataract continued, then he zipped and emerged. 'How does twelve thousand smackeroos sound to you?' I told him it sounded quite well (this was 1973).

He fiddled with his top teeth, some of which he pulled out. 'These phucking teeth are driving me mad . . . twelve thouphand big ones for the righth . . . if I can raithe the moolah.'

Baker raised most of the moolah, and then paced up and down our living room to tell me he was $5000 short. Would I be prepared to entertain the notion (what phrases!) of only taking $7000 and regarding the balance as an investment? An investment, mark you, that could well take off. You know about Melbournians and football. The punters will be beating at the door (hammering at one for effect).

I entertained the notion, unwillingly, and Baker started shooting the following year. The more I watched him, the uneasier I became. First there was the star, the great McCarthy himself: John Jarratt. When some friends and I (to be used as extras) took him out on Wesley College oval for some warm-ups, he seemed to be trying to kick the ball with his knee.

Worse – what I saw being shot didn't seem risible at all. In the novel, McCarthy is persuaded to play the role of Batman in a TV commercial, zooms down from a high window on a cable, and ends up breaking his leg. Baker is cutting and zooming to a frantic TV cameraman trying to capture it for the commercial – but why has he given him a long white beard?

There's a scene where, in hospital, McCarthy makes awkward crustacean love to a woman similarly plastered. Baker, not content with the usual opportunities thus provided, adds a fart or two to add to the merriment.

I only learned of this latter embarrassment when I visited Tim Burstall a few months later. Burstall had bought the rights to my third novel, *Let's Hear It For Prendergast* (fortunately he never got to making a movie of it). He asked me if I'd like to see some reels of *The Great Macarthy* (Baker even got his name wrong). We sat at his editing machine, I put my mug of coffee on top of it, he pressed a button, and the coffee whirled everywhere. Some of it seemed to drain into the machine's innards. Would *Macarthy* come out in sepia?

After profuse apologies, I watched some sequences of Baker's movie on a little screen. Then I looked at Burstall, and Burstall looked at me. 'It's only a rough cut,' he consoled. Can a fine cut transform a rough cut? With a director whose idea of comedy is false beards and farts?

A fortnight later, I went to a preview at the State Film Centre. Before the initial credits rolled, it was excellent. After that, it was not. Humiliated and unable to bear it, I left before the end, only to be pursued by the director. 'What's the matter?' he called as I fled the foyer. 'What have I done?' He'd turned a comic novel into a witless farce.

Reading goes down well

Once one becomes well enough known as a writer, the art or craft can be given up and one can coast along merely being one. The non-writing life began for me when in March 1972 I did a reading and speaking tour of the New England Tableland. Some kind of reputation must have preceded me, because I was carefully chaperoned by a polite but firm man with a German name from the University of New England. Whenever I appeared to be enjoying myself mingling with audiences after the readings, he would gently suggest last drinks and escort me to my motel.

If my performances could generally be described as successful, in Glen Innes I was a sensation. On a warm evening in a church hall, my chaperone told the dutiful audience who I was and what I intended to speak about – the writing of comedy. The moment I opened my mouth in order to do so, a large sub-tropical insect flew into it, and they got a practical demonstration instead. Unable to speak, I mimed a need for water and gulped some down, sending the insect plunging down my oesophagus like a barrel going over Niagara Falls. It proved easier than expected to croak about the subject with something paddling around in my stomach, because the audience were already in fits.

I have also taken creative writing classes. 'Workshops get things moving,' wrote one enthusiast in a writers' magazine, 'unblocking something like a gentle laxative, releasing that inner demon that needs to get out.'

I have coaxed that inner demon out of aspirants, only to sometimes have a lot of trouble coaxing it back in again. I have listened to participants reading out their efforts and have strained for compliments, worrying that I was falsely raising their hopes. If you're at a workshop to enjoy yourself, stretch your imagination and discuss things that Australians don't normally talk about, that's fine. But real writers don't go to them. Real writers know they have a lot to learn, and that they can only learn it on their own.

There were compensations. Once, when I was reading a passage from D.H. Lawrence's *The Rainbow* to a group at a summer school in Toowoomba, I noticed one woman in tears. The passage described the death of Ursula's father, Tom Brangwen, by drowning. ('He fought in a black horror of suffocation, fighting, wrestling, but always borne down, borne inevitably down. Still he wrestled and fought to get himself free, in the unutterable struggle of suffocation, but he always fell again deeper.')

The woman was elderly, and came from the Queensland country town of Chinchilla, where she'd had a hard farming life. She asked me later how to get hold of the book, and I directed her to the college bookshop. The next morning she told me she'd stayed up most of the night reading it, and – in tears again – how sorry she was she'd come to the experience so late.

Inspired, she then wrote stories of her early farming life, stories so simple and moving that instead of the usual sympathetic murmuring that followed a reading, there was total silence. Techniques of writing can be taught, but nothing will teach him or her how to dream. This lady knew, exactly.

Around this time, the Department of Adult Education at the University of Adelaide organised a Young Writers' Workshop, with the poet R.A. Simpson, the novelist Peter Mathers, and me. It was held in an old mansion in the fishing port of Goolwa, close to where the Murray runs into the sea.

In one corner were the rebels, led by John Forbes, who composed his poetry, and his truculent questions, enveloped in a fine mist of dope, and regarded the tutors with amused condescension through rimless glasses. The tutors preferred alcohol, and drank every night at the Goolwa pub, and then celebrated the workshop's end by touring McLaren Vale vineyard in Peter's car. Inflamed by a wine tasting at the last one on our itinerary, he drove at full speed at a huge mound of grape mulch, which exploded all round us. 'Grapeshot!' he roared.

This was unwise preparation for the Adelaide Writers' Week that followed. I had a college room at the university and Peter did not, so he moved in with me. Five minutes after the light was turned out he started snoring, and continued for most of the night. The next night, around one o'clock in the morning, I woke him up with a shout. Disturbed in the middle of some complex dream, he ran round the room crouched over and mumbling, then went back to his camp stretcher and continued snoring where he'd left off.

Since this was the day of my talk, I disturbed him again, apologised, and evicted him to the back of his station wagon. I've been in situations where the audience was fighting sleep while the speaker remained alert, but I had the opposite – a wide awake audience and a speaker who'd had two nights without sleep. 'You were good on Balzac,' the publisher Bob Sessions said to me afterwards. 'Pity you didn't pronounce his name correctly.'

Later in the week came a second ordeal. Peter and I were relaxing in a restaurant when we were told that the great American novelist John Updike's keynote address was to be broadcast live on Radio National, and four writers were needed on stage to ask questions and act as literary potted palms.

An hour-and-a-half later we were sitting facing a couple of thousand people in Festival Hall. I can remember nothing of Updike's eloquent address, but every detail of what happened before and after. Updike, understandably nervous, asked me where the men's room was, and I like to think my directions were lucid and pointed, even witty. Later, when he'd finished, the chairman turned to the uncomfortable quartet: 'And now, questions.' First, writer A. 'No. No questions.' Writer B.

'None.' Writer C? 'No, nothing to ask.' I didn't have any either, but this collective incapacity to question was being broadcast all over the country. So I manufactured one, asking him whether he thought magic realism (it was new then) would be the fictional way to go. Updike seized on it with relief, and Australia's honour was saved.

Three o'clock in the morning

Peter Mathers himself was a magic realist before the phrase was invented. His novel *Trap*, which won the Miles Franklin Award in 1967, was one of the first to move an Aboriginal character (Jack Trap) in from the fringes of Australian fiction. His second, *The Wort Papers*, is a wildly inventive account of two generations of the Wort family, with scenes of comic genius.

When we moved to Sydney Peter was a regular visitor. He liked to drink, smoke and tell stories. Some were on the tall side, but it didn't matter. His tales were not so much highly coloured as imbued with the fantastic – they took on an imaginative truth.

One night, when he called in after an outback adventure, he claimed that in western Queensland he'd seen 'an appetite of wild pigs' crossing the road. He got out of his car, gave chase, and brought down a young one with a tackle, only to be menaced by a large sow. A bottle or two later he returned from our bathroom claiming to have seen a cockroach the size of a small dog, and wondered whether it would rear up and bark at him. Later still – Peter was a three o'clock in the morning man – there was music and dancing, and two of our sons came up to complain that plaster dust was raining down on them 'like confetti'.

Sometimes, when we were in Melbourne, we'd visit him. He lived in what seemed a conventional brick villa on Richmond Hill, under a huge Pelaco sign. Once the door was opened, the contrast was total. Visitors had to twist and turn down a dark hallway whose walls were covered in paintings to reach the living room, where towers of books rose from every flat surface.

His kitchen was a vitreous museum of preserves, bottled from his vegetable garden, which was as densely packed as the house. One night – at three o'clock in the morning – he led us out to it. With the ice palaces of the city shining in the distance, he dug up a copy of *The Wort Papers* and extolled its virtues as compost. It had been remaindered, and he'd bought up a bulk lot and buried them.

In the 1980s Peter wrote plays, and in the nineties his vagabond imagination turned to sculpture, and he created a series of demonic figures from bread and plaster. Some had to be redone before being exhibited because weevils had got into them. These edible artifacts sold well, and one of them stares at me as I write. And in it I can see the wildness of Peter, who went sixteen rounds with pancreatic cancer in 2004, until finally he couldn't get up again.

Sooty boiler

In the early seventies, Melbourne (at least to Melburnians) was considered Australia's cultural capital, and though we felt an intrinsic part of it, we decided that was precisely the time to leave; and in February 1976, after an enormous farewell party, we did, and headed for London.

Our good friend Clare Forbes, at the time married to Cameron Forbes, the *Age* London correspondent, had been hunting for weeks for a house where the rent was modest but the space large enough to accommodate five children (one would briefly stay behind). The task seemed impossible. Then she hit upon the idea of making me a professor. 'Professor Oakley? By all means, madam. I'm sure we can find something.' They found a big house in profoundly unfashionable Peckham, opposite Peckham Rye, where William Blake claimed to have had a vision of angels.

We arrived at Heathrow at eight o'clock in the morning, twenty-eight hours out from Melbourne, where, our house sold, furniture farmed out to friends (piano and roll-top desk never to be seen again) we'd slept the last night in bare rooms on mattresses, in transit already. As we approached Heathrow customs, one of our sons put on his white mummy mask and peered up at an unamused official through his one unbandaged eye.

Peckham Rye has a peculiarly English grottiness – rows of blackened tenements curving away into nineteenth-century mists. Our place is a genteel island, with central heating and Liberty wallpaper. When we turn the heating on, there is a pungent smell of gas. I ring the company, a man comes, lies prone, then makes an announcement. 'You've got a bad case of sooty boiler. I'm declaring this a Dangerous Appliance.'

Three days after our arrival it snowed. First a random sawdust, thickening to torn Kleenex. It snowed on the cars and the common, on the three-wheeled milk van, the bingo club, the broken glass along the top of the primary school wall. Our kids threw it, kneaded it into shapes and brought it inside to show us. It was like freezing bakers' dough, and made the bones of my fingers ache. I had the chill Emily Bronte feel of England in my hand.

'Excuse me,' said Mr Tate, headmaster of Peckham Rye primary, 'is there something wrong with your boy?' He asks me this in a stuffy overheated corridor, where I sit squeezed into a tiny desk outside Kieran's classroom. I explain that he is new to the country and to the school (his first), is having trouble adjusting, and won't let me out of his sight.

We're all having trouble adjusting – to numbing cold, funny little packets of tea, butter, biscuits and soups, strange meat cuts at the butcher's (neck of cow), vests instead of singlets, plimsolls instead of sandshoes, iced lollies instead of icy poles, American whisks instead of straw brooms, and rats under the stairs.

One morning, Carmel runs screaming from the downstairs lavatory. There's a rat swimming in the bowl. Eugene, who's ten and good with animals, extracts it expertly with fire tongs. I take it over to the common in a plastic bag, release it, and as it attempts a sluggish escape, stone it to death. The nearby bus queue watch astonished. The borough of Southwark has a ratcatcher, who introduces himself at the door. He smells powerfully of alcohol. Will he just breathe into their nests? He is friendly, calls me squire, and sprinkles blue powder at strategic points.

When summer comes there's a heatwave, with the temperatures reaching an unprecedented ninety-five degrees. On my way into town to meet the writer and academic Ian Turner, the bus overheats and we break down. As we wait for a relief bus, an Alf Garnett voice yells from down the back: 'We're stuck here while those buggers in Westminster sit on their arses and do nothing about it.' There are cars stranded in the streets, and people lying stripped to the waist in parks, exposing pale English flesh. London suffers a collective heatstroke.

Short theatrical interval

Some time later I see Ian again, for lunch at the BBC cafe. He's with the actor John Bluthal, who's in what he calls his meet-the-manager suit, a brown pinstripe. Bluthal seems to know everyone. 'See that guy over there? James Joyce's nephew. Hi Val!' he shouts. 'That was Val Doonican.' He tells us of the meanness of the great Jewish writer Isaac Bashevis Singer when he was behind him in the queue. 'The rice puddink is 35p? Forget it.'

Bluthal wants to know about the Pram Factory. 'These people,' he says, after I describe it to him, 'have got the wrong idea. Theatre is all about top billing and private dressing rooms. To hell with numb bums and bad coffee.' He has stories about the early days of Australian radio, when there were often no rehearsals – you were just given the script and did it live, being careful not to read out the stage directions. 'As I did once,' he says, then roars into an imaginary mike: 'I'll kill you phonerings!'

Bluthal invites me to a rehearsal of a play he's in at the Haymarket, so I can learn how things are done here. I sit in the cavernous, empty theatre and watch Trevor Howard wander the stage as if lost, fluffing lines and missing cues. He's drunk. When they pause for a break, the director comes down to me and asks if I'd mind leaving.

'You really shouldn't be here,' he says.

'Couldn't agree more,' I manage, making for the exit.

Three plays are written while in London: *The Ship's Whistle*, about the preposterous literary personage Richard Orion Horne, friend of Charles Dickens, who migrated to Australia (failed at the Pram Factory, successful in Adelaide); *Buck Privates* (overseas success if you count New Zealand); and *Scanlan*, a monologue that Max Gillies turned into a hit. But in the meantime, a three-year literary grant wasn't enough to support a large family renting a large house. We were dependent on interest from the invested proceeds of our Richmond house sale.

Frozen family found

When winter comes round again (we'd only just seen it go) the interest cheques arrive irregularly, and as Christmas approaches none arrive at all. Nervous days are spent waiting for the postman. Each time the front door's sphincter rattles we rush to the hallway: Christmas cards and bills, TV Rental threatening removal if payment not forthcoming, the gas company demanding money forthwith.

A box-less, gas-less Christmas! The central heating failing, our breaths condensing, real frost on the tree, our movements slowing until in the new year we're found, kids glazed in wrestling positions on the carpet, mother wedded to the stove, father's fingers fixed around a biro writing a last message. Time to cross Peckham Common and face the bank manager.

An Australian, asking for an overdraft? Again he peers at me. Things are worse than he thought. It's the socialists! Spend, spend, spend! And it's going to get worse before it gets better! You'll see dole queues the length of Rye Lane!

Yes, yes, yes. Take the money and run – to the shops! All Southwark seems to be Christmas shopping in Rye Lane; the South Londoners, cloth-capped, pouched-and-pink faced, shrewd cockle eyes behind National Health glasses – unchanging, untrendy, the service people who clip the tickets, a world of bingo and Wimpy bars, almost as far from Kensington as Soweto is from Johannesburg.

We take a groaning bus to Hamley's, the greatest toyshop in the world – five floors packed with people and toys. Then we stand in the bus queue with games, plane-building kits, a glowing yellow Frankenstein's monster and a whoopee cushion, while little old ladies with hatpin tongues wait behind us, ready to race past. Here comes the Number 12, and here they come from behind. We form a phalanx and clamber aboard. A termagant is forced back and yells abuse, then with a volley of afflatuses (a son is playing the cushion like an accordion) we lurch forward.

Just like home

In the new year our remittances arrive, three at once, so we buy a second-hand Volvo station wagon. The travel urge stirs again in my wife – now that we're settled – and we go on expeditions. She does the planning and the driving. I do the navigating and worrying.

We do Cornwall, the Cotswolds, Scotland, Carcassonne (a remodelled nineteenth-century Disneyland, where the pensione sheets hadn't been washed. I complain, but what's the French for pubic hair?). We couldn't get accommodation in the beautiful village of Domme in the Périgord as we'd planned and at nightfall had no choice but Milhac, perhaps the world's dullest hamlet, at the very bottom of La France Profonde, where the locals, who spoke the language so slowly even we could understand them, stared at us mystified: why would anyone holiday here?

In the depths of La France Profonde.

Memorably, we did Ireland. Five kids wanted to come, so in the station wagon we had to go across and up. Us in the front, four smaller kids in the back, the biggest positioned laterally behind them, cases in the rear and on top in two storeys.

The Volvo was then pointed toward the ferry port of Fishguard, but it behaved like an overloaded camel, and we lost time. When we crossed into Wales, it started raining, and the cases had to be covered with plastic sheeting which, in the wind, turned into a spinnaker. Whey-faced villagers laughed and pointed as we tacked in and out of the breeze, and we reached the port just as whistles were sounding and the loading bay about to close. After a rough ride over the Irish Sea, with our kids placed along the side to accommodate their vomiting, we arrived at Rosslare. The sun hadn't set, even at half past nine in the evening, and as we headed south-west down deep green lanes it flashed out at every turn. Little did we know that it was saying goodbye to us for a week.

A soft, misty, intangible rain began and the next morning, after we'd overnighted at Clonmel ('known the world over for its bacon') it had set in. The Rock of Cashel materialised out of it, as if it were floating on its hill. The ancient seat of the kings of Munster, with a lonely tower and high ruined roofs, it was burned by Fitzgerald, Earl of Kildare. When upbraided by Henry VII of England, he excused himself by saying, 'I thought the Archbishop was in it.'

Ireland seemed like the end of the world to the Romans, but I felt completely at home. The places we drove through were like Australia's provincial towns, except for the inhabitants. The people in the rain-soaked streets spoke in accents so musical it sounded like recitative. And in the pubs it turned into bel canto.

We spent a week in a village called Myross Squinch, welcomed by Margaret, a crimson-cheeked landlady, in yellow beanie and gumboots. Our cottage was modest, but not when compared to the tiny stone one nearby where, Margaret told us, she had grown up with fifteen brothers and sisters.

She also said that the English family who had rented the house before us had gone home early. One Sunday they'd seen a group of men hurling balls along a side road. It was a local game, a combination of boules and bowls, but the English thought they were practising bomb-tossing and left.

At night the inhabitants emerged from hibernation and

gathered at the local pub. It was presided over by an enormous ancient who, though it was only nominally summer, scorned a shirt or a singlet. We were welcomed, Guinnessed, and invited to sing our national anthem. Hoping to be let off, I said we didn't have one. The tent of flesh replied that we did indeed, and if we wouldn't sing it, he would. An accordion whined from a dim corner, and 'Waltzing Matilda' was rendered to applause.

Our cottage had an unusual feature. Every time our bedroom door was opened or closed, a fine shower of paint specks fell like dandruff from the ceiling and our children soon looked like lamingtons.

At the week's end, we drove up to Dublin in the rain. In the 1970s, Dublin was definitely not swinging. We had a terrible meal of grey fish and green chips, inspected the Book of Kells, and made the mandatory pilgrimage to James Joyce's martello tower in Sandycove. We breasted the parapet and felt the wind coming off the sea. We were standing on the spot where, on

Carmel and Josephine go Irish in the wilds of Connemara.

16 June 1904, his novel *Ulysses* begins. How did Joyce manage to turn this bleak and uninspiring prospect into something as reverberant as anything in Homer's *Odyssey*?

Later we retreated to a couple of spartan rooms in Donnybrook, a suburb that could have been transplanted from Melbourne. I took out the tourist map, and as I said the rippling place names to myself – Knockaboy, Kilcormac, Cloonbannin – I realised that 'Ireland' is a fiction, a lyrical and lilting lie. The Irish have bemisted their sombre land with a gossamer web of language. Ireland should be heard and not seen – it's all talk, all wayward and wonderful words.

Large rubber clothes peg

By June 1977, with my grant running out and a wife and six children to support, it was time to go home – not to Melbourne, where we had many friends, but to Sydney, where we had few. Why? asked some of the former, puzzled as to why we could abandon depth and intensity for the sybaritic and superficial. To quote Fats Waller when someone asked him what was so good about jazz – 'If you gotta ask, you'll never know.'

At 7.30 on a morning in August, the caravanserai leaves Peckham in two cabs for Heathrow, where we're told the flight has been delayed seventeen hours. We make camp in various corners of the terminal, and at 3.30 next morning we leave, feeling jetlagged already. By the time we reached Sydney we were vegetables. But when I manhandled the gigantic trolley out of the airport, the warmth came at us like a greeting. We were jobless, but all things seemed possible. There was something narcotic in the atmosphere's blandness; soon I'd be unaware I was breathing it in.

Then we crossed the bridge, with our kids (now down to four – Madeleine, our eldest, opting to stay in London and Justin, our second, preferring Melbourne) and sixteen suitcases, to a flat my agent Tim Curnow had found for us. We had it for six weeks, while its occupant, a well-known Australian writer, was in the south of France. I'll give him anonymity (he's dead now) because two of our kids found a bedroom drawer containing erotic photographs and what was either a dildo or a large rubber clothes peg (which is how I described it to the narrow-eyed and suspicious children).

It was only mid-August but the sun shone and Manly beach beckoned and the kids rushed over the road to it, like long-leashed dogs suddenly released. They ran, they yelled, kicked sand and paddled. Then there was the excitement of the ferry – the spray and the seagulls, the heeling of yachts, hydrofoils getting up on their hands and knees and gathering speed – and at night the Luna Park ferris wheel like a huge starfish, sparkling, as if just lifted out of the water.

We found a shabby bungalow in Bondi Beach. I was still in culture surprise – the low frontier skyline, the liver-brick flats, dragonfly TV aerials, the Neanderthal lope of the surfies, with their waterlogged blue eyes, the sagging fences, the who-cares beachfront shabbiness. Carmel's response was to paint the kitchen, despite my protests that we were only renting. It was done in Chinese red, which made the cockroaches look infernal. Never, especially if you're from London or Melbourne, go into a Bondi kitchen in the middle of the night. Turn the light on and the whole room seems to move.

There was also the Australian workman to get used to,

after relative English deference. After we'd unpacked, there were so many boxes out the front of the house it resembled a fortification. There was a knock on the door early the following morning. It was the dustman, in navy-blue shorts too big for his skinny legs and a singlet bulging like a spinnaker in the wind. 'Fair crack of the whip, mate,' he said. 'You'd need a bloody pack of camels to move that lot.' Naturalised at last.

We were running out of money fast. Plays of mine were going on in Melbourne and Adelaide, but I couldn't crack it in Sydney. One day, Max Suich, editor of the then-feisty *National Times*, met me in the pub for a drink and offered me the job of theatre critic. I tell him I'll think it over, but he knows I'm bluffing. When I leave, he calls out after me: '*National* theatre critic.'

Before I decide to take it on, I go one night with the playwright Alex Buzo to see Patrick White's *Big Toys*. The director concentrates on externals (flashy Sydney décor) while the central weakness is untouched – the working man (Max Cullen) adrift in a comedy of manners. He stands there lost, as if he'd blundered in off the street. 'What did you think?' asks Alex afterwards. 'Terrible.' He agreed, but added that if judgments have to be made, a facade should be preserved 'to prevent knocking'.

Facades? Knocking? Favouring the local product? Was this what I'd have to do? Once you become a drama critic, writers, actors, directors – people you'd known in the theatre – regard you differently. You've gone over to the other side. People say nasty things to you at parties. Did I want to end up like Harry Kippax, standing alone and unsmiling in foyers? I took the job.

Joining the enemy

My first review – I have the Dead Sea scroll still – appeared in the *National Times* for 28 November 1977, and it was of Harold Pinter's *No Man's Land*. Here's how it ends: 'Stewart Chalmers as Foster and Tom McCarthy as Briggs are soundly cast, but as Spooner, Alexander Archdale is not. It is not too much to expect an actor of his experience to modulate his reading into a lower key, so that we'd have the chilling Pinter chamber music at its best.'

That absurd headmaster's tone! The augustness of the admonitions, the guarded dispensing of compliments! It wasn't just Alexander Archdale who needed to lift his game; it was me.

The next week I flew to Melbourne to review a play by Richard Beynon – not *The Shifting Heart*, his best-known work, but another, which I've forgotten. But I remember the flight back to Sydney. A gale was blowing. We'd taxied out and stopped, and as we waited, we rocked. We were getting turbulence even while on the tarmac. 'Ladies and gentlemen,' said the pilot from the cockpit, 'we are about to make the fastest trip to Sydney ever – forty-nine minutes. If you're okay, we're okay, and here we go.' After we took off the wind hit us from the side, whacking us with its bear's paw, and we were whipped sideways again and again. Coming down was just as frightening. We lurched and jerked, and our wings flapped like a bird's. After we bounced down into eighty kilometre-an-hour winds, the captain got more enthusiastic applause than Richard Beynon.

I became a neurotic in the air, and a neurotic on the ground. I dreaded first nights. My wife in Sydney, and various friends in Melbourne, soon realised there was no such thing as a free ticket. Afterwards, they'd be questioned about plot points or characters, and sometimes they wouldn't be any more certain than I was.

But theatre critics have to be certain. And for those of them who'd written plays themselves, the problem was worse. Because they know they were about to witness a production that had been shaped and honed, in which every movement, every nuance, had been considered. Months of writing and weeks of rehearsal have come down to this frightening moment: triumph or turkey?

Usually neither, a mix – a triumphant head on a turkey body, with feet that work but wings that don't – and exactly what kind of creature that emerges shining out of the dark it's the critic's job to determine.

I was bearable to sit with reviewing the classics (I knew the plot) and at my worst with new work, where one must peel back the flesh of performance to find the bones of the script, and then work out if this particular incarnation was doing it justice. For two hours one peers into the play taking X-rays while at the same time pressing the flesh for a diagnosis – doctor and radiographer at once. Watch, listen, scribble, scribble in the darkness, and later find most of it illegible.

All this was daunting enough, but having to review a work by a friend was worse. If you're not a critic you can mumble a few half-truths in the foyer and rip it apart later with your wife. These reviews took me the longest: softening the punches, searching for redeeming features, but also, impossibly, trying to tell the truth.

I lost David Williamson over *The Club* and Alex Buzo (knocker!) over *Coralie Lansdowne Says No*. Would I end up like Bob Evans, who had wine thrown over him, or Len Radic of the *Age*, hanged in effigy in the foyer because of the bad review he gave Manning Clark's *History of Australia*? Or Harry Kippax, dean of them all? I once saw this grim elder statesman lose his balance and cartwheel down the dress-circle stairs of the Seymour Centre, while the two actors in the row in front of me clapped in glee. At last! They were reviewing him.

Certainly the best, and probably the worst, of my reviewing experiences both took place in Adelaide. The best: a Polish theatre company's performance of Tadeusz Kantor's *The Dead Class* in 1978. The dead class was a dead society. Poland was a schoolroom filled with cadavers sitting immobile at school desks, in black, the men in butterfly collars and bowler hats, their faces white, their eyes green-shadowed, as in death.

At the front, presiding, a buxom figure leans on a broomstick under a medieval hunter's hat, a nightmare charlady. At the side of this grotesque tableau moves the director and creator of the play, Kantor, acting as a conductor, modulating the action with subtle flicks of his fingers.

Suddenly the class erupts into life, putting up their hands, pleading for the attention of a teacher who doesn't exist. Some at the back stand on the seats, then the desktops; the class becomes a pleading pyramid. There's no confusion – every movement is orchestrated. It's like a ballet of automatons.

A flick of Kantor's wrist and the class rise, leave their desks, exit, and then return, to waltz music in a grand parade, as the figures bring their childhoods back with them. Each carries a doll-child, black marionettes that cling to their older selves and will never let go.

The classroom is life, where the inmates are condemned to be kept in until the hunter-charlady makes her re-entrance, swinging her broomstick like a scythe: death.

In the program, Kantor defined his work as 'a theatre of concrete reality and not the art of stage illusions'. But in this fusion of gesture, dance, speech and music, concrete reality is left behind. We were in the realm of overpowering imaginative truth.

At the same Arts Festival I had to review a performance of *Oedipus Rex*, the most creative I've ever done – I had to make most of it up. The plan was to attend the opening of Writers' Week at the Orlando Vineyards, and then get back for the play. Because of the company and white wine I left late. There was still time, but Dinny O'Hearn, drinker and academic, was driving. He sang Irish songs, and passed everything on the road except the pubs, and as he overtook each car Morris Lurie, the other passenger, shouted encouragement and banged the car door.

Now there was no time left, and more minutes were wasted while Lurie emptied his bladder in the middle of a floral plantation on the edge of the city, his technicolour jacket for once unobtrusive. I got to the theatre after the doors had closed. One was grudgingly opened, and after knocking a row of knees I fell, first into a seat and then into a doze just as the Chorus of Theban Elders were letting loose. I was disturbed by Oedipus and Creon shouting at one another. (Jocasta: 'What is the meaning of this loud argument?') I scribbled some notes, paid attention, then nodded off again, to be jolted awake by Oedipus's roaring as he blinds himself. My review drew considerable praise: 'authoritative' was the favoured word.

Lecturer takes off his clothes

A writer-in-residence is someone funded by the Literature Board of the Australia Council to stay at a university college or some other institution for a couple of months to help students with their writing and perhaps do some of their own. A writer-in-residence is by definition a poor writer. No one would run workshops by day and retire to a cramped room at night unless in desperate need of the modest funding provided.

The most spartan accommodation I ever retired to was at Mannix College, when I was in residence at Monash University. It consisted of a small bedroom and study, both totally bare. I'm out of town, have no car, and the campus at night is dead. Nine weeks of this, I thought, and I'll go nuts.

The college rector, an urbane Dominican, foolishly entrusted me with a key to the senior common room. Depressed by the austerity of my cells, I'd wait for the staff to retire, tiptoe down the corridor, unlock the door, and decant a schooner of red from a cask.

But I was being watched. A portrait of Daniel Mannix witnessed my nightly siphonings, the piercing blue eyes taking it in with amusement. 'Now,' the late but legendary Archbishop of Melbourne seemed to be saying, 'it's my turn. It was you, crouching cravenly over your stolen alcohol, who wrote that play about me for the Pram Factory in 1971, which had me in a bath, in a bed, and in tights in a wrestling ring? Look at you now, your hand shaking over the tap. Straighten your back like a man.'

After a monastic week, Mary Lord, a Monash tutor in English, takes pity on me and allows me into what she calls the literary bedroom of her house, which had earlier accommodated Christina Stead and Dorothy Hewett. I'm saved.

Soon the manuscripts come in. One student, almost blind, feels his way into my office and leaves a playscript. Another offers a short story which has worrying sentences: 'Simon flung an arm towards a corner of the room.' A third, a Chinese student, leaves a long and laborious allegory in which Australia is subtly called Moronia. The poet Chris Wallace-Crabbe, the author claims, has likened it to Swift. What to say to these people? How does one encourage and discourage at the same time? I had to tell the Chinese satirist that there was one problem with his manuscript. It wasn't funny. But other readers say it hilarious, he insisted. He then read out choice passages, having small convulsions while he did so.

'Still not funny?'

'Still not funny.'

'When I famous,' he said at the door, 'I not forget you.'

Mary Lord is preoccupied organising the first conference of the newly formed Association for the Study of Australian Literature, for which academics and writers are converging from all over the country. She is nervous, and has to be fortified by gin & tonics, which she's taught me how to mix.

As well as innumerable lectures, there's a program of readings at the Alexander Theatre. May they be ambushed? I ask Mary. She says they may. I'd written a monologue called *Scanlan*, given by a lecturer who gradually loses his marbles during his address. It was first performed by Tim Robertson at LaTrobe University, Melbourne, where it was advertised as a straight lecture on Henry Kendall, given by a visiting lecturer. For the first few minutes all seemed normal and the students took notes. Then Scanlan becomes erratic, sipping from a hip flask, abusing his audience and taking off his shirt as he heads for a nervous collapse. The most remarkable thing was not so much Scanlan's behaviour as that some of the students scribbled down his ravings almost to the end, including the absurdity 'Blaxland, Lawson and Wentworth, a firm of solicitors, crossed the Blue Mountains'.

And now, in the person of Max Gillies, Scanlan was to be let loose again. Many in the audience – Max had performed the play elsewhere – knew it was an imposture, but not its victim, A.D. Hope. During a somnolent reading by the eminent poet, a manic figure scurries onto the stage, thumps his briefcase onto the table and ferrets for his notes. Gillies apologises briskly, hustles the bewildered figure from the platform and launches into his lunatic lecture (it was one he was to give all round the country, playing to packed houses wherever he went). There's enthusiastic applause – from everyone except Frank Moorhouse, who gets far less, and complains that I cheated by bringing in a professional to do what I should have done myself. He sulks for the next two days.

It'll be right on the night

Despite the fact that by becoming a critic I was a theatrical quisling, the Pram Factory politburo agreed to do *The Ship's Whistle*, my play about the inflated English poetaster Richard Orion Horne, who came out to the goldfields to seek his fortune – and as colonial correspondent for Charles Dickens's *Household Words*.

Horne, as keen on physical fitness as he was on pentameters, was made for Max Gillies who, in velvet cloak and top hat, filled the part with the swagger and braggadocio he does so well. The props included an incredibly heavy set of parallel bars, which required six of us to bump up the theatre stairs, and a bust of Shakespeare, which I had to bring down from Sydney on the plane, and which I nursed on my lap.

Flight Attendant: 'Is that a fossil or what?'

'It's Shakespeare.'

'I'll take him up to First Class.'

'With me too?'

'Unfortunately not.'

There were many scenes (too many, I later learned) and a bulky traverse (a wheeled platform that had to be trundled up and down the space according to requirements). The cast have trouble moving it. Barry Dickins, one of the performers, complains that it has run over his teeth, and the rehearsals are rough – normal for the Pram Factory. ('It'll be right on the night.')

I had the usual first-night nerves, and at dinner in Carlton beforehand red wine wasn't enough to quell them. I went into the lavatory, took a Valium and sat on the bowl and waited. Was there an earthquake? The black and white tiles on the toilet floor seemed to be moving.

But it all goes well – the traverse doesn't roll off into the audience, Dickins remembers his lines, and Gillies, riding his ship to the colonies and roaring Horne's terrible poetry, is unforgettable. The old world meets the rough-and-ready new one on the Melbourne docks in the person of Alf the carrier, which I only mention because he's played by the great character actor Reg Evans, who rode his motorbike from Kinglake every night and who later died in the bushfires there.

The hard-to-please first-night audience liked it, and so did the *Age*'s Len Radic – not enthusiastic (when was he ever?) but positive: 'uneven but enjoyable' (how many plays are even?) and 'should keep the Pram Factory audiences happy for weeks to come.'

Alas no. *The Ship's Whistle* was too long and unwieldy (a cast of ten, with thirty roles between them). It closed a week early, maybe because a petrol strike crippled attendances (theatre maxim number one: always put the blame on someone else). But it lived again in Adelaide, where the South Australian Theatre Company did a polished and popular production.

Most boring man in Sydney

My agent, the ever-helpful Tim Curnow, tells us he's moving from his Paddington terrace – would we be interested in renting it instead of him? Probably not, he thought, ' – it's sixty dollars a week, and you wouldn't be able to squeeze in your kids.'

Our kids were down to four and they were squeezed in quite well. And so began nineteen years of inner-suburban life, in what my father, who'd condemned our Richmond house, called 'a tenement'. There's a back lane, where cricket can be played, and where a grumpy old gutter-pisser named Bully lives in a van. There's damp that rises as inexorably as the rent. Each year, I am soon to discover, the elderly landlord knocks on the door, wishes us a happy new year and raises the rent. I then must shake his hand – not easy, since he has Parkinson's Disease, and his hand moves up and down. I must dart mine out to catch his, and then his trembles do the rest.

Twenty-four Renny Street had quite a literary history. Tim Curnow was the manager of the Curtis Brown literary agency, and its office was here. At various times it was visited by Patrick White, Douglas Stewart, Ruth Park and Xavier Herbert. Curnow recalled his wedding party there in 1974, when White gave them a frying pan. Also present were Frank Hardy and Donald Horne. 'They had an altercation outside the dunny, each threatening to stuff the other down the bowl.' And when Xavier Herbert won the Miles Franklin Award for *Poor Fellow My Country*, 'he arrived in a chauffeur-driven Rolls Royce hired by his publisher, Collins. I heard a car horn and there was Xavier sitting up in the back seat like royalty'.

For a while we had calls from writers who thought Curtis Brown was still there. One morning Bob Brissenden was at the door, suited and briefcased. 'I've finished it,' he says. I don't know who was more surprised. I was on a grant and he was chairman of the Literature Board. I explained that Curtis Brown had moved, but despite my pyjamas I was hard at work. 'And I rise at five,' I called after him as he headed for their new address with his crime-fiction manuscript.

For a time, our social life consisted largely of seeing friends who came up from Melbourne, many of whom brought their political intensities with them. Also at this time, I was changing from being an automatic Labor voter to one who could at least entertain the possibility of voting Liberal. I had realised that it wasn't much use having ideas about the redistribution of wealth unless you also have them about generating the wealth in the first place – the engine of capitalism had to be made to work better, investment had to be made more attractive, capital had to be seen as a friend and not an enemy.

At a Darlinghurst restaurant I said these things to an incredulous circle of Melbourne diners: a leading comic actor, a Marxist playwright, and two of our closest friends, a theatrical producer and his then-wife. They attacked me, collectively and individually. It was like a tag wrestle, though I had no one to tag. I remember one of them getting up to go to the lavatory, and tagging his neighbour: 'Give him a go on trade unions.' Enterprise bargaining was a novelty even to the Liberal Party in those days, but I said it sounded a good idea – centralised wage-fixing discouraged investment in new business, and this made unemployment worse. They couldn't believe it. They had an authentic enemy of the working classes trapped at last. When the evening and the shouting was over, the producer's wife called from the door: 'No wonder you moved to Sydney.'

'To get away from Melbourne,' I called back. (Memoirists always have the last word.)

As we got to know people, there were dinner parties – blander Sydney ones. If there were battles, they were personal rather than ideological. At one, the writer Robert Drewe stormed out, saying he'd never speak to me again (he did, although guardedly). At another, one guest thanked me for sitting him next to what he called the most boring man in Sydney (who'd just left). I agreed with him and apologised. Neither of us realised that the most boring man in Sydney had returned to collect a coat and heard what we were saying.

At another of our dinner parties, strange things seemed to be happening. The guests, after enjoying the first of Carmel's delectable dishes, began to look embarrassed. Then, when a firm hand was put on my knee under the table, I looked embarrassed too. Was A touching up B, and C doing the same to D? Then it was the forthright E's turn. Furious, she lifted the tablecloth, to reveal Kieran, touching knees and ankles as part of his own private game.

The most abundant hospitality was provided by the Codys.

John was a publisher, his wife Margaret an educationalist, and at their North Shore house we sometimes met Important People. We saw Clive James in the flesh (which he had then in abundance) as he sunned himself by the pool. Then, when social intercourse became unavoidable, we sat over a salad and white wine. His long comic poem about Prince Charles was doing famously, he confided, and the great German writer Hans Magnus Enzensberger was going to run it in his literary magazine. Once the Germans think you're funny, I attempted, shouldn't one be worried? The sally bounced harmlessly off him. Soon he and his wife rose to go. Was it my fault? I said. Had I ruined the lunch? No, no, said the ever-genial Codys; but I certainly hadn't helped.

On another occasion, at the same house, the Canadian novelist Margaret Atwood put me in my place. I was sitting next to her on a couch. Conversation hummed all around, but between us there was silence. The Principle of Celebrity was operating: she was famous, so she was resting. It was up to me.

'I was one of the judges of the Canada/Australia Literary Award,' I offered. She sat on, pale, freckled and unmoved. I blundered on. 'We've chosen the novelist Leon Rooke.'

She turned her head in my direction without actually looking at me. 'A good choice, considering he was born in South Carolina.'

'But surely he's regarded as Canadian by now.'

'He is regarded by very few people at all. If being known as Canadian was measured in points out of ten, Leon Rooke would rate about four.' A pause, a sip of her drink, some salted peanuts. 'And I'd rate ten.'

Now that we've integrated into Sydney literary life, I'm invited, with two of our larger sons, Miles and Eugene, to play in the annual Actors Versus Writers cricket match. It's organised by Alex Buzo, who takes his captaincy of our team extremely seriously. He's in pressed whites, but his team declines to a motley of browns and greys.

Alex loses the toss and places his troops carefully. I'm in slips, but after refusing to put out my cigarette, exiled to the outfield. Bob Ellis has a toothbrush in his shirt pocket which falls to the ground every time he stoops to gather a ball (a slow process, with the actor–batsmen happily running). Bob has an unusual running action. Only his legs move. The top half of his body is reluctant to do so – it's as if it belongs to someone else.

When it's our turn to bat Alex gives us a solid foundation, but the rest, listless from sun and alcohol, fall away. We lose. He's not pleased. 'You people,' he says, looking at Bob and me, 'treat it as a joke. You wouldn't do that in the theatre.' We protest that it's a bad analogy, but he won't be placated. He's in a bad mood. One of his plays has had a poor reception in Adelaide – a city he hates – and he blames it on 'the frigid Adelaide Establishment and the Carlton Marxists'.

Refuses to get off butt

Here we go again: the Melbourne Theatre Company decides to do my latest effort – *Marsupials*, a four-hander, with Carol Burns, Sean Scully and Max Gillies, with Matthew King condemned to the kind of role actors hate – a walk-on part as an estate agent near the end of the play.

The quartet sit at a trestle table in the rehearsal room and read the script, while there's frantic thumps and shouts from next door – John Bell's directing Shakespeare, and their ranting invades our humble space. I time the reading. To my horror it only lasts sixty minutes. 'Business, old chap,' says Bruce Myles, the director, 'stage business. We'll plump it up.'

A month later, there's a technical rehearsal at the theatre in Russell Street. The lighting designer, a legendary figure, sits slumped and abstracted, a finger deep in a nostril – then becomes suddenly alert, barking instructions to a nervous assistant. Larry Eastwood's swinging wall panels are too heavy, and threaten to revolve unstoppably when the actors push them to enter or exit. Myles curses and blames the production manager, a large, balding man who trips over a briefcase each time he comes down the aisle.

On the Tuesday *Marsupials* opens, I ask Carmel if she'd mind if I sat alone up the back. She's pleased, having had to sit next to my neuroses all her married life. Will the jaded first-night audience laugh at the punchlines? They do. Do they notice the pale backstage arm that sneaks out at every entrance, to stop the revolving wall in its tracks? They don't.

Afterward is always the hardest, enduring the half-truths of family and friends ('loved it'), but this time praise is drowned out by drama. Barry Dickins rushes into the foyer and lunges at me with an upraised bottle of wine. 'You put me in your bloody play!' he shouts. But no way is 'the gummy little poet with the pudding-basin haircut', I insist, him. He's calmed down, lowers the bottle from over my head, I buy him a drink, and we all move on to a supper at Clare and Cameron Forbes's.

But what of Len Radic, Mr Weights and Measures? In the *Age*, Len puts *Marsupials* on his beam balance and finds it lacking in avoirdupois, but audiences didn't agree with him. Then, halfway through the season, when box offices sometimes flag, a gift: 'Denizens of "the end of the world" savage playwright', ran the headline in the *Age*. 'In his latest play', the report continues, 'Barry Oakley calls Carnegie "outer Mongolia", and, in a slightly more charitable moment, "a mean little wooden suburb".' The reporter makes the journey to the end of the world herself and interviews a few unhappy locals. A local real-estate agent is pointed: 'Oakley might have seen more if his nose had not been in the air. Maybe he never got off his butt and made the effort.'

I admit to the reporter that I might have been jaundiced by the fact that my wife and I spent years there bringing up five kids in a cold-water weatherboard, but the publicity is priceless.

Monster escapes

One January day in 1981 Angela Wales, director of the Australian Writers' Guild, rings to say she's worried no one's going to turn up to meet a visiting Yugoslav playwright – could I help? So I go in to the Guild office: a handful of us around the table, with cheese and cask white. The guest is a worn-looking man with a large ginger moustache. With him are two apparatchiks – one suited and smooth, the other with a boxer's face.

The phrase 'cultural exchange' comes into play a lot and our local Marxist playwright is all over them, telling them what a boring middle-class theatre we have here – 'a cash transaction, nothing more'. The apparatchiks nod approvingly, but not the man they're minding, whom I'll call Victor, who gets more and more irritated: 'Don't you think you pay to go in in Yugoslavia?' The local Marxist playwright, taken by surprise, digs himself deeper. 'The law of competition dominates everything in this country. We've got to get rid of the operators and the bureaucrats and get to the people. Get them on side! Show them the realities! Help create socialism!'

'Listen!' – Victor is angry now – 'Socialism *is* operators! Socialism *is* bureaucrats! I live under it!'

'That is not necessarily the case,' says the smooth one. 'Victor is getting excited.'

'I am not excited!' shouts Victor. 'What I say is true!'

'Every society has its faults,' says the smoothie, now getting to his feet. 'You must forgive us, but it is time to go home.'

There was more to come on the international front. Soon after, the Goethe Institute, Germany's cultural arm, announced that there were to be 'German–Australian Writer Meetings'. Some German ones, including the patrician Hans Magnus Enzensberger, would be joining their Australian equivalents 'in a live-in symposium in Kallista, in the Dandenong Ranges, to discuss common problems'.

There were nine of us facing six of them across a huge table. Alarmingly, a microphone was set up in front of each speaker. Every banality was to be recorded. At the warm-up drinks, one of our group asked Professor Reinhard Lettau, a myopic blinker in gold-rimmed glasses, if he'd met any poets during his recent stay in California. 'Perverts?' he said. 'Did I meet any perverts?'

This sounded promising, but it didn't last long. Soon a novelist was inflicting on us a long monologue (translated by Beate Josephi, one of the organisers) about the treachery of writers who give us gratuitous consolation by offering the illusion of order in a chaotic world, which we should be trying to change.

This had been preceded by a frightening morning where each of us had to explain, to the tape and the table, what we do and in what context we do it. Context was the big German thing, so if one wrote novels one was expected to give a brief history of Australian fiction. Since drama sounded easier, I focused on that, because there wasn't all that much of it.

The next day we were permitted to stop worrying about literature and go on a bush walk instead – though this was objected to by a tubby, bearded anarchist playwright called Federspiel, who seemed to be here on sufferance. 'Fuck Nature!' he shouted, and stayed behind and sulked. The rest of us set off into Sherbrooke Forest in search of lyrebirds. The Germans, their well-cut overcoats draped over their shoulders, proceed carefully (snakes? spiders?) in a blue haze of Gauloise smoke, and relish the crystalline purity of the air. Our guide creeps forward through the bush, holds up a hand, and we pause – to take in, right on cue, a lyrebird's lilts, leaps, cascades and gurgles, as every bush bird is mimicked.

That night, songs around the piano, with the poet Fay Zwicky at the keyboard, 'Waltzing Matilda' is played and sung, and its status as Australia's unofficial national anthem explained. 'Now it's our turn,' says Lettau, whose complexion has become inflamed after a couple of drinks, and he sits down and plays 'Deutschland Über Alles'.

'That is ours,' he says.

'Many people' – I had also drink taken – 'don't like that song.'

Lettau looked up at me, face and gold rims gleaming. 'I yam sick of professional anti-Germans.'

'I don't like the words.'

'You don't know what they mean.'

'A lot of people in the last war,' – it's out! It's mentioned! – 'knew only too well what they meant.'

Beate taps me under the table to desist, and I do, but the monster has been released, and I feel as if I'm dragging the whole conference down around me, though we shake hands and the subject is changed.

Then it's open day, and people come up from Melbourne and gather on the lawn in the sun, including the reporter Jan McGuiness who, to my horror (the monster has escaped the building!) puts the little upset in her *Age* diary the next morning. It has become The Incident. Then a man called Benno comes up and says, 'I hear you are an outspoken Australian writer. Can you answer zeez questions please for ze German press agency?' (The monster has left the country and is heading home!) I tell him there's no story – simply a misunderstanding – a nothing.

'A mountain, how you say, out of a dunghill?'

'Quite.'

On the last morning, I apologise to the gathering. 'A misunderstanding,' says the novelist Judah Waten, repository of Jewish wisdom.

'No, no,' says Hans Magnus, the prince in the cream linen suit. 'You took us from the said to the unsaid, which is where

Judah Waten ponders a takeover at the German–Australian Writers' Meeting. (Photograph John Tranter)

these conferences should go.' Enzensberger, who's deferred to by his colleagues in a way unimaginable in this country, has spoken, and that's that. Federspiel, the fat anarchist, who's been bored the whole time, is now more bored than ever. 'I haff a question,' he says. 'Ven iz lunch?'

Censorship is back

Can you discuss literature out of existence? Workshop plays to death? Soon after this Teutonic talkfest, there's a playwrights' conference in Canberra, where promising plays are workshopped, with professional actors, directors, and curmudgeons called dramaturgs, whose job it is to make script suggestions that the writer almost certainly won't like.

As a dramaturg I scored, amongst others, *The Butterflies of Kalamantan*. The problem was that its author, Jennifer Clare, was a highly experienced actor who knew more about the business than we did, and didn't hesitate to let the actors, the director Alison Summers, and me know it. During the first rehearsal she leans over to me and says, in a stage whisper, 'That's not the way I want it done, darling.'

The deficiencies in the script seem obvious, but Clare can't see them. Alison Summers – 'you're obviously new to the business, darling' – becomes upset and leaves the room afterwards in tears. A reconciliation meeting is arranged in the bar, but Clare, in black top, black slacks, dark glasses and resplendent silverware, represents unanswerable experience, against which both Alison and I seem powerless, and the play's problems are never sorted out. Give me a theatrical naif any time.

Boozing, backbiting and occasional bonking are normal at playwrights' conferences. What made this one special was a seminar on children's theatre, in which the woman representing Sydney's Nimrod Theatre formalised political correctness into commandments: you shall not show racism, sexism or classism in a favourable light; you may not reinforce stereotypes; you are not to write about issues (uranium mining, the killing of whales) unless you search for the causes behind them; you must not use outdated forms unless in a novel way. Worse, all this nonsense was corroborated by Alan John, Nimrod's reader of plays for adults, who warned that an author might be required to draw out the implications of his or her work.

The listeners, many of them writers, sat there and took it, which provoked me to launch an attack. Neither of you, I said, seem to understand the nature of imaginative writing: good plays tend to work by implication – bad ones are didactic. You object to censorship from the right, while applying it yourselves from the left. Ron Blair got to his feet and backed me up, but the rest remained mute. Maybe they were stunned (or wanted their work performed).

It got worse. We witnessed a performance of *Sex and Violets*, by a dapper and elderly Bob Herbert, which featured a skeleton, subtly called Deadie. Halfway through the interminable work, Deadie suddenly drooped forward, as if it too, like the audience, was falling asleep. It wasn't a success, but there was no need for what followed in the discussion. Neil Armfield announced that 'the play embodied attitudes that were offensive and distasteful', which left poor Bob, up on stage, blinking under his black eyeshade. Then Armfield administers the coup de grace: 'It should never have been put on.'

The Australian National Playwrights' Conference of 1981

spelt out what many knew implicitly: the days of censorship were back, but now they entered stage left.

Writer disappears

Meanwhile up north, at Griffith University, Brisbane, another kind of miasma was descending on literature, its sinister messages encrypted in impenetrable jargon. Try to get to the end of this: 'It is useful to consider that the laborious accumulation of currently possible signs of verisimilitude is always undertaken within the operative criterion of a regime of signification, that is within historically determinate conditions of intelligibility of these signs. However, the notion of conceptual paradigms raises questions in its own right, given its possible representations both as a deep structure of biography and as a totalising principle identified with some general cultural unity or mindset.'

This, and pages more like it, was written by David Saunders who, at the time, 'lectured on text discourse' at the university, and it was he who met me at Brisbane airport when I was invited to be writer-in-residence there. It is taken from a collection called *Griffith Papers on Biography*, which I regretted not having read before accepting the appointment. I was going to a place infested by semioticians and deconstructionists, where the word writer was put in inverted commas.

Saunders, a tall and sombre South Londoner, explained to me as we drove to the campus that at Griffith they cut in sections across the disciplines, which seemed to suggest an absence of roots. Andrew Field (biographer and friend of Vladimir Nabokov) told me later the result was that there were no disciplines at all. The semioticians had left him isolated; the only communication between him and the rest (he was a professor there) was by notes left in pigeonholes. They theorised about biographies while he wrote them. He was working on one about the writer Djuna Barnes, and carried the manuscript around with him, hanging from his wrist by a leather strap, as if the semioticians might savage it.

I was given a comfortable office, and left to puzzle over why they would invite someone to take up residence whose creative function they didn't believe in. Field, whose isolation induced sensitivity to these things, warned me about the thinness of the office walls, and he was right. Frightening phrases from next door tutorials came through – frame analysis; proxemic behaviour; intransitivity – from my adenoidal English neighbour. I was trapped in a Malcolm Bradbury novel.

I was here, to use their jargon, to provide epistemic difference: a fall-guy in residence. Innocent biographers were also invited, including the American scholar Deirdre Bair, whose Beckett biography had only recently appeared. In a seminar, she told us that in the course of her researches she'd met a niece of Beckett's, who asked her if she'd clean out a cupboard, which was filled with rubbish she'd one day get round to burning. Bair unearthed a shoebox of Beckett's letters to his friend Thomas McGreevy at a crucially unhappy time in his life, and was so affected she 'went into the bathroom and vomited'.

What were these Griffith kids being taught? I went to a lecture by the professor of philosophy, another American, and was appalled enough to take notes. His subject was Institutional Determinants of Text Production, in which we got a cartoon version of the conflict between Galileo and the Catholic Church: 'Galileo beat the pants off the Jesuit theologians, and then stuck his finger in the eye of Pope Urban VIII. So the Pope brought down the hammer quick smart . . . let me write some of those words up here for you – papacy, theologian, Jesuit . . .'

At another lecture, Herbert Grierson's famous *Night Mail* documentary was shown, with script by W.H. Auden ('This is the night mail/ over the border/ bringing with it/ cheques and postal order'). The lecturer's theme was neither the visual nor verbal language, but how the production patronised and exploited the working classes. In literature, nothing was studied before the early nineteenth century, because that marked the beginning of working-class awareness. When I asked one student why she didn't do Shakespeare, 'We don't do eighteenth-century writers,' was her reply.

In the words of another visitor, an engaging professor of literature called Callahan, from Portland, Oregon: 'Man, don't talk to me about all this bullshit – I can't take another word of it. These kids are being sold a bill of goods.'

The students at the University of Queensland were luckier, and I escaped there as often as I could. The University of Queensland Press was my publisher at the time, and wanted Bernard Hickey, a visiting academic, to launch their edition of two of my plays. 'Academic' goes nowhere near describing Bernard. 'Manic leprechaun', Desmond O'Grady's phrase for him, is closer.

Bernard lectured in Australian literature at the University of Venice and approached his task like an evangelist. Everything, and everyone, was wonderful. There were the wonderful Oakleys, the wonderful Fosters, Tranters, O'Gradys, and anyone else connected with the subject.

Bernard's Venetian hospitality was indeed wonderful, as we discovered in 1975. He'd found us a pensione, taken us to regional restaurants and once to a party at a palazzo, where he'd rushed at various notables as if to attack them, and then finally cornered the hostess – 'The Countess Loredana,' he shouted at us, emitting a delighted giggle, 'translator of Patrick White!' He was unfailingly kind to visiting Australian writers, who sometimes rewarded him by putting him into their fiction (or in my case, a play). He was irresistible material.

Bernard agreed to launch the book of plays, and didn't let us down. Dressed in an outfit of belted denim with flaps and buckles at the breast pockets, he resembled a portly package. He pronounced the slim volume unequivocally wonderful, and likened its author to the Latin satirist Juvenal.

Andrew Field, the author, and the Vice-Chancellor of the University of Queensland bemused by Bernard Hickey's garment.

Bernard, a man whom it was impossible to dislike, had developed an Italian attitude to what he called 'the authorities', and made regular visits to Australia to cultivate them. He told me after the launch 'it was of particular moment' that I'd had a conversation with the university's vice-chancellor, and that this at all costs should be followed up. Was it about your work? he asked. I told him that it wasn't. I'd learned that the vice-chancellor had flown in one of the ancient Swordfish biplanes that crippled the battleship *Bismarck* in the face of withering fire. His regard for me was as nothing compared with mine for him.

There had to be a confrontation with the Griffith semioticians, and it came near the end of my stay, when John O, another staff member, gave me a goodbye dinner. Mike Harris, my office neighbour, was there with his wife, one or two others and, fortunately, Callahan, so I wasn't totally outnumbered. We were three drinks in before hostilities commenced.

It was up to me to open the bowling. 'These kids you're supposed to be teaching – they don't even know about the Renaissance – and one of them thought Shakespeare was an eighteenth-century writer.' Mike shook his head wearily and gave me a patronising smile. 'We look at structures, not periods. It's not who did the writing – it's how it's constructed.'

'Jesus,' said Callahan, 'constructed. Are we talking building sites or what?' Mike was still smiling, but now it was an irritated smile. What tiny teeth he had!

'Social forces construct the writer, and therefore the work. You're way out of date on theory.'

Callahan was getting angry too. 'So tell me this – this writer here. Why'd you invite him, when you don't believe in writers?'

'Yes, we do. Who's better equipped to explain the forces that shape him than the writer himself?'

The table had gone quiet, and they now looked at me. 'You've got it all arse-up,' I said. 'A good writer is exactly the opposite – someone who transcends these forces.'

Mike looked at me pityingly. 'Bourgeois individualism I'm afraid.'

The bourgeois individualists left shortly afterwards. As we went back to our college rooms in a taxi, both of us a little the worse for wear from alcohol and argument, Callahan told me he'd had enough.

'I'm getting out of here,' he said. 'Man, you want to hole up in your room then do the same. Get out. Before you think and talk like they do.' (I survived, did my nine weeks, and came home.)

The glass house

Leon Fink, investor, patron of the arts and property developer, had bought Kinselas Funeral Parlour in Darlinghurst, and there was a party to celebrate. I wasn't invited, but tagged along with people who were. As the invitees were urged to wear something black, it was obvious from my Gold Coast white trousers that I wasn't one.

The central feature of Kinselas was an art-deco chapel with a non-denominational altar, backed by a fresco of ducks winging into the sunset. Behind the altar someone had found a cross and a Star of David on long sticks, which could be mounted according to the religion of the deceased. In front of it a band was playing. Many of the guests wore frangipani on their necks or ears, and spent much of the time rushing at one another for an embrace. It was all very Sydney, and after a few free drinks I felt more and more Melbourne and went home.

Months later, the place emerged transformed, with a bar and

two restaurants – a theatre one on the top level, and a proper one on the ground floor. Graeme Blundell brought in classy cabaret acts for the former, and Tony Bilson ran the latter, with the chapel – now a dazzling miniature cathedral of glass – at its heart. Kinselas soon became Sydney's most popular rendezvous.

When we could afford it, we drank or dined there, and when we couldn't, which was most of the time, John Timlin, friend and now my agent, would celebrate his winnings on the track by shouting. Eventually the whole building became a performance space where people liked to be seen.

Sometimes you didn't have to leave your seat: theatre would come to you. Once, while I was dining, probably at Timlin's expense, Max Gillies, made up as a posthumous Bob Menzies for an upstairs revue, waddled over to us, his angel's wings shaking as he walked, and addressed me in lordly fashion, suggesting it might be wise if I left, since I wasn't going to pay. Ripostes were useless. Actors in costume were invulnerable.

Publishers were more generous then, and the University of Queensland Press launched *Scribbling in the Dark*, a collection of my articles and reviews, in the Kinselas sanctum. In keeping with the theatricality of the place, my friend Dick Hughes did the job in a black Christian Brothers habit, and threatened anyone who tried to slip out without buying a copy with an impressively large strap. 'Horne,' he said, 'face the front.' (Had Donald ever been spoken to like that before, except by Frank Packer?) Amongst the bemused crowd watching all this was George Melly, the English jazz identity and friend of Hughes's, dazzling in a pixilated suit. Was this how books were launched in this country?

More theatre: the Australia Council was dining one evening in the crystalline temple, and we were urged to peep in. Its director at the time, Timothy Pascoe, was being farewelled. He was lying on the table, blissfully smiling, eyes closed, perfectly dressed as always, with a lighted candle on his chest, as if he were being prepared for the mortuary rather than retirement.

Occasionally, when the writer Judah Waten and his wife Hirell were up from Melbourne, we'd eat with them there. The last time we saw them, the doorman, a large body under a top hat, was having trouble with a drunk, who kept making runs at the entrance, which were forcefully repelled. On his final run, Oddjob grabbed the drunk, slammed him into a post, then swept his top hat off and bowed us in.

Judah, though looking as always like a member of the Politburo in his sombre suit, had lost his hearty ruddiness and didn't seem well. Diabetes, Hirell said. 'My doctor told me I was not to drink, smoke or have much to eat,' added Judah. 'He said even then you may not live longer – but it will seem longer.'

He then began an anecdote which I've forgotten, and as it turned out, he had too. He built up to the climax, then came to a stop. There was an awkward pause, during which the abused and abusive drunk staggered up to the window behind him and let loose a huge chunder against the glass. Neither Waten saw it, and, not wanting to interrupt, we listened as Hirell finished the story for him. Soon after, the Kinselas' windows had a half-curtain of velvet to shield the in from the out-crowd, and not long after that Judah died and Kinselas did too, sold by Leon. The great days were over.

Meets someone else

Late in 1981, after so many good times – conferences, workshops, residencies, so much drinking and discussing what was literature and what was not (and actually doing so little of it), something happened that made it all seem of no consequence. Carmel, whom I'd so often left behind with the children while I was off pondering more serious matters, decided she'd had enough. She returned from Melbourne (where she'd been researching the life of the painter and teacher Dattilo Rubbo for her university thesis) and announced she'd 'met someone else', and was leaving me.

Writers are the world's greatest recyclers, and since I've gone over it elsewhere, there'll be only brief reference to it here.

In depression, one becomes susceptible to portents. I had a powerful attack when I went to the Australian Writers' Guild Christmas party at The Stables Theatre. Friends were sympathetic. 'Get yourself a new outfit,' said one. 'Could be a play in it,' offered another. 'You're looking fine,' lied a third, peering in at me, the bags under my eyes pendulous from sleeplessness.

We're drinking and smoking and talking when the allegory attack begins. A derelict comes into the foyer and slumps against one of the sofas. His jacket is half over his head, his back is bare, and he has a cut lip. Angela Wales, director of the Guild, tells me it's William D, a writer and Guild member, in the grip of the alcoholic horrors. When the playwright Clem Gorman later led a group of stayers towards King Cross, D tried to follow. He reeled, fell across a planter box, got to his feet and did his best to keep up, as though fearing if we got out of his sight he'd die. Depressed, narcissistic, I thought that would soon be me.

By March I was running out of spirits and money. Max

Suich (I hope not out of pity) gave me regular book reviewing for the *National Times*, and Vic Carroll (looking, but certainly not sounding, a little like Billy McMahon) offered me a fortnightly theatre piece in the *Sydney Morning Herald*.

For my first effort for the *Herald*, I interviewed the bellicose Miriam Hampson, who'd been running the New Theatre in Sydney's Newtown since 1948. Miriam was tiny and tough – her steel-grey hair seemed like an extension of her personality. She swore like a wharfie, with a voice almost as deep.

She led me into the shabby little auditorium, and we squeaked into old cinema seats. They were doing yet another production of *Reedy River*, Dick Diamond's folk musical from the 1950s. The coolabahs up on stage looked tired. Miriam was already talking: 'When in doubt, do *Reedy River*. Frankly, I'm sick of it, but we need the fucking moolah – don't print that.' She paused for breath. I darted in to ask how she managed running an amateur theatre for so long.

'Later, later. I was just thinking of the time Les Tanner – or was it Keith Gow? – got his foot stuck in a chamberpot in *The Lion on the Square*. Clumped around the stage trying to shake the fucking thing off while the audience fell out of their seats. Or the time whatsisname, that fat actor, stamped his foot, broke the boards, fell into the rostrum he was standing on and gave the rest of the fucking speech from inside the bloody thing.'

'But wha—'

(Raising her hands.) 'Later, later. What was that fucking play we did in 1968? *America Hurrah*. There's a man and a woman inside these huge dolls, and they, if you'll forgive the expression, copulate. We knew there'd be police in the audience, so we had all these fucking big wharfies lounging round the exit. At the end the actors waddle off and out the exit to get away, ripping their dolls off as they run. The cops get up to go after them, but the wharfies block the fuckers.'

'And wha—'

'Are you interviewing me or am I interviewing you? We scrounge, dear, that's how we do it. Laundromat does our costumes for nothing, hardware lends us doors, poke about Reverse Garbage for props. We're not rich enough to go broke. I'll show you last year's figures if I can find the bloody book. Memory's fucked ever since I got mugged – don't print that.'

'Here in Newtown?'

'In fucking Bellevue Hill, thanks very much. A guy goes for my purse, I hang on, and I hit my fucking head – don't print that. Where you from?'

'Paddington.'

'I knew it.'

Shirtsong

Everyone has a special shirt. Mine, a slightly regrettable pink, had buttoned shoulder flaps and breast pockets for maps, which is why its mail-order makers called it the Airline Pilot. It was a man-of-action shirt. My wife, now back with me after a separation of five months, said it suited me. I shaped it and it shaped me.

So when in June 1982 the screenwriter Keith Thompson suggested I apply for the position he was leaving – head of the Writing Workshop at the Film and Television School – I wore it for the interview.

Thus shirted, I found the confidence to tell the panel the

truth – that I'd written only four screenplays in my life, and only one had made it to the screen: an adaptation of my play *Bedfellows*. Another CV plus, I added, was that I did not write the screenplay for my novel *The Great McCarthy*, which David Baker had turned into a total turkey.

Subtly, pinkly luminescent, I was so self-deprecating that the panel came to my defence, reminding me of my achievement in other writing fields. I nodded, but doubted that made me suitable for the job. Here was a man, they must have thought, so confident in his abilities that he'd spent the entire time diminishing their importance (and he looks as if he can fly an aeroplane as well). They gave me the job.

I wore my magic shirt when I first met the students, and self-deprecated even more. They listened, trying to conceal their bewilderment, while I told them I rarely went to movies – give me books any time.

Since one can't wear the same shirt every day, a lot of bluffing was required. Film's a technical minefield, and the possibilities for solecism were endless. At a lunch with my boss, the small and sharp Richard Thomas, he complains that the production people have been slow in replacing video with film, and I give a knowing nod. At a table with a group of students sitting reverentially around the famous English director Lindsay Anderson, one of them praised his 'great tank work'. (Had he done war movies?)

'What's the noise?' I ask my assistant Chris Fitchett (who knew far more about film than I did – he'd even made one).

'Tape hiss.'

'Of course – very annoying sometimes.' Richard Thomas, who by now was getting suspicious, sat in the chair opposite my desk, looked at me hard, wondered whether students should start off with a day using the Portapak – or would a Super Eight be better?

'Good question. I'll have to think about that.'

The AFTS was generously endowed by the federal government, so the students were taught in small groups – tutorials rather than classes. The one-year screenwriting group was more tolerant of me, since I'd been on the panel that chose them. Under their guidance I worked hard to catch up, reading about narrative structures, plot points, montage and back stories, and watching films they recommended in the school's theatrette.

The three-year students were another matter. These were worryingly talented people who found it hard to conceal their puzzlement that I had the job. (I agreed with them.) They included Jane Campion, who submitted a screenplay with a large phallus as a frontispiece, Paul Hogan (soon to re-style himself, for understandable reasons, P.J. Hogan), and Ian David, later to make a name in television.

In my second year, still hanging on, the pinkness of my shirt fading fast, the Film School scores a coup. Linda Agran, big-wheel London TV producer and script editor of *Minder*, has agreed to be In Residence for a few weeks. First Class, thanks. Her reasoning is pithy: 'If you think I would even consider spending twenty-seven hours with my knees around my ears paying for drinks and picking at trays of mystery meat, you've got the wrong bloke. Also, I love flying like I love dieting and Margaret Thatcher, so if I am going to die I am going to do it at the front end, wearing my little free socks, pissed as a parrot.'

Three weeks later she arrived, pushing expensive matched suitcases. She was short and dark and wore large sunglasses. She's taken to the Sebel Town House. Considering the temptations of first class she seems quite sober, and immediately calls for two bottles of champagne. Principle one of TV production, she says – hold your liquor. She fronts up to a dinner at a Greek restaurant the following night, all make-up and blazing eyes, and soon has the one-year trio – Chris Lee, Steve Wright and Billy Marshall – in thrall.

The commercial TV channels court her. The head of one offers to collect her from the school in the company helicopter. The head of programming of another invites her to his mansion for the weekend. It has a suit of armour on the stairs, she tells us later, that lights up as you pass, a tennis court, and a swimming pool that can change colour.

Agran closets herself with her trio of admirers and says, 'We are going to create a TV series, and we're going to get it to air.' I pick up some of what she says from the next room: 'The English language is a millstone around a writer's neck. It makes them think of dialogue, and not structure. Don't go from script to visuals. Visualise the scene first, then write it.' (Why haven't I thought of that?)

One day, while they were huddled over their project, I took a phone call in my office. 'Is that Mr Marshall?' a voice barked. I told the voice I'd get him. Billy picked up the phone and seemed to quiver. Fred Schepisi, he scribbles on my notepad. 'Yes, Fred. No, Fred. Yes, Fred.' If Fred likes Billy's screenplay about Lasseter and the golden reef somewhere in central Australia, he's made.

'It's a definite maybe,' says Billy afterwards, still quivering. I told him not to get too excited – in the seventies, Schepisi had a habit of taking novelists to lunch, intoxicating them with wine and promises, and nothing would happen. He did it to John Hooker, who arrived at our place so drunk he could barely stand. 'Fred's going to do *Jacob's Season*,' he managed, before collapsing on the couch. And he did it to another novelist, who also collapsed on the couch. 'Who was that?' asked Billy. 'Me.'

Billy went back to his huddle, and a TV series did in fact emerge. It was called *Stringer*, about, inevitably, an alcoholic journalist who reeled from crisis to crisis and filed irregularly. With Agran's backing, a commercial channel picked it up. It made little impression – and, according to Billy, the English lead actor was 'a pain in the ass', but it was made, a feat unheard of from three one-year screenwriting students.

Then Linda Agran had to go. In return for the hospitality she'd received, she gave the school the original *Minder* submission – the story outlines and the characters that George Cole and Denis Waterman would bring to life. For the school library, it was like *The Book of Kells*. Then she struggled into her tracksuit ('Christ, I'm as fat as a goose') put on her sunglasses and flew away.

My time was running out too. After eighteen months of bluffing, I decided to take my incompetence elsewhere. I was getting older, and job opportunities diminishing. But before I risked the next step into the unknown, my CV suddenly improved. A man from Foreign Affairs with the oxymoronic name of Bruce le Compte rang to say I'd won the Canada/Australia Award.

As seen on TV

The Canada/Australia Award gives the recipient a modest sum and the opportunity to eat, drink and read one's way from one end of the country to the other (in alternate years, it enables a Canadian writer to do the same here).

Since my visit coincided with the grandly titled Harbourfront International Festival of Authors in Toronto, I started off there, where one does one's best to appear to take for granted the presence of famous writers, while at the same time having furtive peeps at them. I try hard not to look at Salman Rushdie, who sits in a corner of the Hilton Hotel Reception Suite, aloof, five o'clock-shadowed, heavy-lidded, like a Mughal prince.

At dinner, a reunion with Elizabeth Jolley, who tells the company she'd had to ring the housemaid to find out how to use the bathroom tap. Elizabeth, always playing the naif, confused and out of place, maddeningly humble and apologetic, lost in the big world.

Rushdie lets us know what's happening up in the dome of the pantheon: 'I was having lunch with Calvino when we learned that Garcia Marquez had won the Nobel. Italo (Italo!) thought it outrageous it hadn't gone to Borges, who'd invented magic realism in the first place.'

It was whispered that it was still possible that the blind, all-seeing Borges might come, but it's a no-show – the supremely important don't bother to descend at all. Still, there was Ted Hughes, forelock over forehead and prognathous of jaw, and J.P. Donleavy, white-haired and layered in Irish country-squire greys, with the comic novelist's inevitable air of loss. And wasn't that Derek Walcott over there?

Rushdie dazzles us with his talk. The provost of Cambridge when he was there was an innocent old bachelor, who told the students at the beginning of the year: 'You may think you'll learn a lot in the lecture room. But the most important work will be in each other's rooms at night, fertilising each other.'

The readings over and the crowds (700 to every performance) gone home, in poor shape (Seagrams, a sponsor, had left a bottle of whiskey in each writer's room) I started out on my cross-Canada tour. At Halifax, the last leg of my flight to Newfoundland is cancelled because of crosswinds at St John's airport. But Eastern Provincial announces that if anyone's interested, they're still going in. A few take up the offer – most do not.

'These guys,' says a flight attendant to a woman even more nervous than me, 'they're bush pilots. Crazy guys. Fly when no one else does.'

To calm us, they hand out free drinks. But it's tricky. The attendants are smiling as we come in to land, but they're hanging

Thinly overcoated in Newfoundland.

on to their straps, white-knuckled and tense. It's close – I can see the wing dip dangerously low as we touch down, and when we make it the pilot gets applause.

It wasn't hard to be a celebrity in treeless, rocky St John's, so I was invited out to their breakfast TV program. It was hosted by a silver-haired smoothie named Broph, who was, as my escort put it, 'kinda slow'. He had one of my books – the plays launched by Bernard Hickey in Brisbane – and opened it at one titled *Marsupials*. The native creatures it dealt with were publishers and writers. Broph thought it was about kangaroos.

'Tell us about these animals in your play,' he said. I explained that these animals were involved in alcohol and adultery.

'We get enough of that here. Kangaroos, where's the kangaroos?'

'There aren't any.'

'Tell us about them,' persisted Broph, refusing to give up.

'They hop and they eat grass, and that's about it.' Broph wound the interview up with, 'That was the visiting Australian writer Barry Oakley, and his *Marpusials*.'

At Halifax – on the way back now – wartime convoys used to gather in the harbour, I was told, before crossing the Atlantic. I was taken to St Paul's church where one can see 'the silhouette of a clergyman imprinted on a window by the great 1917 harbour explosion, when munitions ships blew up, resulting in the biggest man-made explosion until the atom bomb'.

There was Montreal, there was Ottawa (a painfully stuffy lunch put on for me by the Australian High Commissioner, who hadn't the slightest interest in writers from his own country or anywhere else), and then Calgary, which, as the novelist Mordecai Richler once noted, looks as if it's just been uncrated. I gave the usual reading to the usual dutiful crowd, saw an enormously fat Siberian tiger at the zoo, and, at the museum, tins from Sir John Franklin's expedition to find a Northwest Passage (it was the lead poisoning from the tins that killed them). Then something even sadder: a subdued group of Sarcee Indians being shown their own traditional artefacts – magnificent headdresses, a huge tepee like a basilica of animal skins – by a white guide, telling them about their own lost culture.

Then over the Rockies on the Canadian Pacific to Vancouver, where the local writers told me it was no use going out to Dollarton to pay my respects to Malcolm Lowry (*Under the Volcano*) because his beachfront shack had burned down and there was nothing left to see. Finally Vancouver Island, the warmest place in Canada, which had been brought to life for me by the novelist Jack Hodgins, then San Francisco, and then, with my foie somewhat gras, home.

The entire instrumentarium

'Writer/Producer – ABC Radio Drama and Features.' That sounded promising, though I had doubts about the producing side. Since my old one had gone the same colour as my hair, I got myself another pink Airline Pilot shirt. If I combined its man-of-action map pockets with the Canada/Australia Award and the fact my radio play *The Great God Mogadon* was that year's ABC entry for the Prix Italia, I was in with a chance.

I glowed, I deprecated, I joked. ('What is it about this position that attracts you?' 'I'd be able to walk to work.') I got the job. On my first day in the excrement-coloured building in

William Street, where Drama and Features occupied a floor, I was put on display at a staff meeting, then led to a bare office.

Shan Benson, a friendly, rubicund man in green shirt and cravat, came in soon after and gave me something called the Lewis Packer file, which contained a series of letters of increasing vehemence from a man who hadn't liked the way his radio play had been edited. 'Step carefully with freelance writers,' he said, and left me with the file. The letters started with the producer, worked their way up the bureaucracy to Leonie Kramer of the ABC board, then went down again, with threats like the following: 'Matters of breach of contract will be pursued with your legal department, although that department seems to believe the ABC to be so sacrosanct that a mere writer must accept ex cathedra claims of mortmain.'

Ron Blair, ringing for the deputy head of the department, Julie Ann Ford, but getting me, tried to calm my apprehension about the technicalities of radio production. 'All you have to do is make sure the actors don't pop – just keep an ear out for their plosives.'

But the following day I went into one of the control rooms to watch the technically gifted Andrew McLennan. He sat at a jumbo-jet control panel directing a group of actors below us in the studio like a Qantas pilot. The play was a typically complex drama by David Foster which required orchestrating a dizzying variety of sound effects. It was as if I were to learn how to play piano by watching Glenn Gould play Bach.

I continued to sit in my office, working on a play about the painter Danila Vassilieff, who built a house of massive stone blocks at bohemian Eltham, on the outskirts of Melbourne – but I can't be the writer and not the producer indefinitely. Dick Connolly, head of Drama and Features, calls in on me (perhaps to see if I'm still alive) and creates slight alarm, by saying I'll have to take over the high-culture *Radio Helicon* program, his pride and joy, later in the year. Dick's a great language man, a lover of Latin, and asks whether I've read the new Seneca translation. Not as yet, no. Did I know that there's a Latin word for the opposite of apotheosis, translatable as pumpkinification? (Maybe it's happening to me.)

Early in May, on the day our son Kieran has to go into hospital to relieve the pressure on the graft on his arm from his scalding accident eleven years before, I have to attend a radio seminar at the Goethe Institute. Kieran is now thirteen, and we've given him a Walkman as a treat. He's very grown up, and says he's not scared as Carmel takes him to hospital. She tells me later than he even managed a joke as he was trolleyed into the theatre – 'Will I see pink elephants?' We go back in the evening to see him, bandaged and brave, his arm zippered with fifty stitches. He begs for a Cherry Ripe, and we say not yet. But he has to have it, and then vomits it up over the sheet.

The cultural anschluss (my second after Kallista) is run by a German acoustic maestro called Peter Leonhard Braun, who would be happy to give advice to those brave enough to play their tapes for him (I still didn't have any).

First up was the maddeningly confident Tim Bowden, who had the office next to mine and whose door carried the following souvenired notice: 'Grand Hotel Cairo. Will Guests Requiring of Partners for Sleeping Purposes Male or Female Please Most Kindly Request the Desk of Reception.' Bowden played one of his tapes of interviews with prisoners of war of the Japanese – a series of moving and beautifully edited stories, with one elderly Australian voice seamlessly coming in after another.

Stories like these: 'McLusky, a terrible talker, finally died, one of hundreds. As we were lowering him into a grave his body bends, and there's this explosion of breath from where the head is. "Christ almighty," said one of the burial party, "you can't shut the bugger up even when he's dead."'

Who couldn't be moved? Who couldn't laugh? Radio's von Karajan pondered and then pronounced: 'Your narrator's voice is too cold for the subject.' Cold? What on earth could he mean? 'I vill prove my point.' He plays a tape about an appalling World War I battle at Armagnac, which he says is still remembered all over Germany. There's a memorable sequence in which one of the men who tend the graves was digging a well, and comes across, six feet down, a soldier, intact, sitting with his rifle between his knees. But Braun's narrator's voice is too dominant. Speak up and say so? No.

Who'll be the next victim? Kevin McGrath, of ABC Education, plays his tape about the notorious actress Susannah Cibber, against a background of the conflict between classical Italian and English ballad opera in the eighteenth century. Sounds okay to me, but the maestro is shaking his head. 'Zat is transport radio. You are trundling the information from A to B. It is museum radio, it is dead radio.' Kevin, a diminutive man, seems to shrink further in front of us. 'I cannot accept it. Though I admit your copulations (he means links) were effective.'

Back in the office, Tim Bowden was encouraging me. 'Sooner or later you're going to stop writing scripts and start producing them. There's nothing to it.' So finally I had to come out, cross the road to Forbes Street, enter a control room, and look down through the glass at the actors awaiting their instructions in the vast space below. They were going to do one of my own scripts, about the aeronautical pioneer Lawrence Hargrave, with Neil Fitzpatrick playing the part.

When the technical operator asked where I wanted the microphones, and I said 'the usual', he nodded knowingly, briefly bluffed by my shoulder straps and map pockets (I was winging it in my Airline Pilot shirt) – this chap can't be bothered with technicalities – and off he went.

When Hargrave had to demonstrate his rubber-band-powered flapping-wing model flying machine, the sound effects girl scraped a piece of fibreglass rhythmically with a stick, and it sounded exactly like fibreglass being scraped with a stick. Later, when Hargrave is supposed to be levitated by his box kite, Fitzpatrick got up on a ladder and yelled his lines over a tape of wind, and it sounded like an actor up on a ladder doing just that. Lawrence Hargrave never flew, and neither did my first radio production, and if the ABC ever decide on a re-run, don't miss it.

I'm put in charge of scripts. Complaints about some of Shan Benson's rejections now went to me. Harry Reade, the shorts-and-thongs rough diamond who drank at breakfast at playwrights' conferences, was particularly irate. 'Who's the fool who rejected it?' he roared down the phone from a superbly Queensland address (83 Caladium Street, Gumdale). 'I know why. It's about Aborigines. I grew up with fucking blacks in shacks in Shepparton and I'll write about them how I fucking well want.'

I had the radio on during my rejecting duties, and I was lucky enough to pick up another Queensland opinion on the subject.

Interviewer: 'The Aborigines were here before the Bible was written.'

Sir Joh Bjelke-Petersen: 'Well, who knows what it was, when they were, or when their religion? Can you call that a religion, worshipping something or other that's dead or something like what you were saying, the spirit of the goanna?'

I truffled amongst the scripts for hidden treasures. Musical themes were popular: 'Herr Beethoven, no orchestra could play this "music" as you call it. Speak to me! Are you deaf?' From a feature on Handel, getting increasingly impatient with a singer: 'Not like that, you silly waterhead!' And lines with a powerful sub-text, from a play about Magellan: 'Captains Mendoza and Cartagena have left the ship, and now there's a whole boatload of seamen heading for Concepcion.'

Geoffrey Whitehead had recently taken over as head of the ABC, and one lunchtime the radio staff gathered to meet him. Pasty face, shaded glasses, funereal suit. Bowden, sitting next to me in the airless studio, wasn't fooled for a minute. After Whitehead had come out with some rapid-fire platitudes about the value of radio, Tim got to his feet and asked: 'What radio programs, in the course of your listening, appeal to you in particular?' Whitehead goggled, paused, smiled, and retreated behind a translucent shower of words.

As well as this big meeting, there were lots of small ones. It's how bureaucracies function. At one, the future of Drama and Features was discussed. Because of its unyieldingly highbrow programs, it existed in a permanent state of budget uncertainty. But the audience figures were alarming. For Sydney, 3000 was considered average for *Radio Helicon* – the program Dick Connolly, its founder, wanted me to take over. For *Wednesday Play*, an asterisk, which meant its Sydney listeners were below a thousand. We seemed to be huddling around the dying fires of high culture.

It was my job, when I moved into the Helicon office, to keep the flame alight. I was in charge of the department's flagship:

two hours a week of high-protein culture. I was visited by postulants. Eric Waite, a small, sallow man in an ill-fitting blue suit, told me he had tapes containing new material about Xavier Herbert – how his wife Sadie hated him, and how he'd had an affair with Dymphna Cusack.

I green-lighted that one (as they say in Hollywood), as well as an interview by Ann Whitehead of the descendants of the William Lane New Australia settlement in the 1890s in Paraguay. The accents were as if preserved in amber, with a lost Australian purity about them. But I'd also inherited commissioned scripts which I had no choice but to put on. Did anyone want a feature on Dr Johnson's life of the poet Cowley? Or the sonnets of Petrarch? Or a painfully detailed description of the objects on the French writer Georges Perec's desk?

Was it any wonder that the announcer Peter Young, after introducing the Helicon program for the night, would go round to the control room and watch *Minder* on TV, returning just in time to read my continuity with an enthusiasm that suggested he'd been enjoying *The Rhetoric of Cicero* the whole time?

Though I was technically in charge, it was Dick Connolly's fiefdom, so I took a risk by committing cultural adultery one night when he was away – I programmed a mini-rock opera by James Griffin, and sat at home enjoying its irreverence, while expecting an angry phone call at any moment. Later, Dick and I had it out. 'Do you see Radio Helicon as something totally sealed off from popular culture?' His reply was tart: 'Listen – people tune in to get away from popular culture.'

Dick had a thing about German radio, and a year after our first Teutonification, we had another. It was run by Klaus Schoening, balding and all in black. He demonstrated something called *Hirschspiel*, a combination of words, sounds and music – in short, as he put it, 'the entire instrumentarium' in order to create 'acoustic documents'.

We sat and listened politely to yelps, hisses, groans, songs and speeches in impenetrable German. Still, his English was entertaining.

'Is your ABC station a monopole?'

'We are, in a sense, historigans.'

'We must develop a new granma of acoustic signals.'

After all this, Keith Richards, our man in Brisbane, was foolhardy enough to play a tape – a monologue by an overnight porter in a run-down hotel. It was dismembered in front of us. 'No, no, not like that! It must not be *about* reality – it must *be* the reality. You must create radio – phonic tooth – like this: he pressed a button and released an orgy of chanting, yelling and drumming.

'This isn't *about* the conquistadors' savagery in Mexico,' he shouted above the din, 'it shows the thing itself.' The actors declaimed repetitive lists of ugly German words for Kill! Maim! Rape! Burn! with increasingly percussive force, hammering the listeners into the ground. We tried to follow it in an eccentric translation: 'Go and catch the old animals and grind them into a fine powder.' (And what the hell was *gliss*?)

In the stunned silence that followed – 'You are shocked I see and you are meant to be shocked' – Schoening said he regarded the play as a the greatest radiophonic work of the century, adding that it was greatly appreciated by a Prix Italia jury 'which consisted of eight critics, eight blind people, and one with a single eye only'. (Laughter.)

'I am sorry, but I intend not a joke.'

Back in the office, we're told there's a computer course now available (the thing's in a cardboard box waiting to be let loose), and Shan Benson and I are the only ones who haven't enrolled. He's retiring soon, and so, I hope, am I – though to what? Who will save me, proven incompetent in both film and radio? Our weekly $300 salary usually lasts till the day before payday, which means twenty-four hours of careful husbandry. 'Last night, like a squirrel to his eyrie' – as recorded in my diary of the time – 'I took up to our bedroom, away from the appetites of the boys, one third of a pint of milk, six slices of bread, three Vita Brits and an apple.'

The inward sleep

There is, or was, a god and his name was salty, pungent Max Suich, at the time chief editorial executive of Fairfax newspapers. I'd written to him, putting out feelers for work, and now he rings, and asks what I'm looking for. I tell him. He says he'll get back to me. Eighteen days go by (I'm counting), and in a procedure not unlike K's attempts to get through to the authorities in Franz Kafka's *The Castle*, I start ringing, but get no further than his secretary.

Then there's a week's relief from radio and from waiting – a tour of the Richmond/Windsor area with Olga Masters, sponsored by the National Book Council. Our job is to read our work before selected groups of victims, and then become victims ourselves. We kick off before a deathly silent class of schoolgirls, then an equally silent group of English teachers. It was as if we were reading out obituaries.

Then came workshops. We ran the first together. Olga's policy – she's a modest, hesitant, good-hearted woman – was to encourage everything. She has an unusual way of starting. It seems to take a few seconds before her mind slips into gear. We listen to a strange remote lady reading a strange remote poem. I've been through this before, and have developed the technique of the inward sleep. On the outside, I seem to attend. On the inside, I sleep quietly. The poem is incomprehensible. I am silent afterwards, Olga ('Your – yes – poem – I – very good – ') warmly encouraging.

A delicately boned English lady reads a story that includes the sentence: 'Jack jerked himself back to the present.' I dared not look up. The strange, remote woman, having been encouraged by Olga, turns to prose, a story about a man who feels 'a warmth and hardening in his groin' every time he starts a fire. After starting one in a dress shop, he has trouble escaping through a window 'because of the condition of arousal he was in'. Eyes down again.

Olga presses on, praising everything. When I say goodbye to her, the workshops thankfully over, she says she has headaches and trouble focusing. Her headaches, and her sometimes awkward progress through her sentences, mark the beginning, I later learn, of a brain tumour that will kill her.

When I get home, Carmel tells me Max Suich has rung – could I ring him Monday? When I do, he says Robert Haupt, the editor of the soon-to-be-launched *National Times on Sunday*, the *National Times* re-invented, wants to have lunch. 'Theatre reviewing,' says Max, 'your old trade.'

This is good news – I'll cease being a burden on Drama and Features – and bad: it's a job I need but don't want. Could I go over to the other side again? I'd had an eight-year break from scribbling in the dark. My spirits rose – if this is possible – and sagged at the same time. I was becoming quite good at getting jobs I'd rather not have.

'Fuck it,' said Robert

There was no one else at the restaurant where Robert Haupt and his deputy editor Valerie Lawson said they'd meet me. A fire was burning. I chose the table carefully – a three-seater. If I chose the right chair, one of them would have to sit beside me – depriving them of the psychological advantage of my having to face both of them. They came in, and pleasantries were exchanged. Robert inspected the wine list, and ordered an expensive white. He tasted, paused, and found it good. We all drank, and it was indeed good.

More pleasantries. The food arrived, and was presented with ceremony. Robert ordered another bottle. I struggled with Tasmanian scallops in a pastry that Leo Schofield would have found too hard. Robert was editing a schnapper, and Valerie excavating half a lobster.

I was counting his drinks. I had a strategy. Get him half-under before money is mentioned. We had each now put away five glasses. Robert's crinkly black hair had freed itself from the top of his head and was hanging over his right temple, like a wig that was about to come off. Valerie remained inscrutable behind tinted glasses. She was beginning to laugh for no reason. I was becoming flushed. The second bottle disappeared.

Robert ordered champagne, at an unthinkable price. Would the gentlemen like cigars? The gentlemen would. A box of Havanas was presented, and two neatly decapitated. Wait. Wait for the champagne. Wait for him to have a glass. We paused, we puffed.

'Okay,' said Robert, who'd become slightly dishevelled, 'what are we looking at?'

'That depends on what you'd like me to do.' There was a

feeling that Robert had more or less forgotten what he wanted me to do. He was on to his second champagne. I stayed with my first.

'Twelve hundred words a week,' said Valerie, who was holding her liquor better than either of us. 'How much would you want?' Awkward silence. Crackle of fire in the corner. Robert was becoming distracted. Look at him, not at her. I leaned forward slightly to catch his eye, which was fixed on a blond at a nearby table. We puffed again. The cigar was ambrosial. Don't do the drawback. Don't have a dizzy spell. I needed to go to the toilet. Robert needed another drink.

'Excuse me while I phone my accountant.' It wasn't funny, but they both laughed. While I was relieving my bursting bladder, Robert, I hoped, would be having another champagne. I'd planned to ask for $300 a week, but decided to think big. When I returned, Robert's wig-like coiffure had slipped further down the side of his head. I was a trifle unsteady. Robert's nose, always impressive, was now glowing.

'I was thinking of $400 a week.' Silence. Absurdly high? Laughably low?

'We were thinking $350,' said Valerie, who, now that moolah was mentioned, had regained her native cool. Robert was looking away. He seemed not to care. Everything stopped. Who'd weaken first?

'Fuck it,' said Robert, '$400 it is.'

I poured him the last of the champagne, while he made a feeble protesting motion. I liked Robert. A man after my own liver. I puffed, without doing the drawback. He puffed, and deeply inhaled. His eyes were glazed. He was having visions.

'We're going to build you up as the only national critic. If there's an important play opening in Melbourne or Brisbane or

Adelaide, you'll go there.' Pause. I should've asked for more. Too late now. 'We've just given TAA a big newsprint freight contract. I think they'll come to the party.' When I get up, will I fall over? Robert did, years later, in a New York restaurant, while doing a deal with his publisher over a book on the Soviet Union; with a glass in his hand, his heart would stop, and he'd fall backwards in his seat, dead.

Rat remains on sinking ship

First up, in Melbourne, I got two turkeys, but some high comedy in the street. *Spook House*, at St Martin's South Yarra, was so bad the actors looked embarrassed taking their final bows. Near me, Len Radic and Helen Thomson were scribbling away for the *Age* and the *Australian*. 'How long have you been a critic?' Helen, surprised, asked afterwards. 'About two hours,' I said. I'd joined the freemasonry of critical coroners, who hasten away while the corpse is going cold to write their reports. Was it killed, or did it die of natural causes? It was a gloomy business.

Kill Hamlet, at the Anthill Theatre, a cold hall in South Melbourne, was even worse. The program gave due warning of what was ahead: 'The spectator should sweat in a theatre without armrests.' Germany was declaring cultural war on me yet again. An actor prowls around the small, freezing and terrified audience, commenting and confronting. 'And you, sir, yes you, you will come out here and be a tree?' I sat there and sweated – will he see me, furtively taking notes? True to my inflexible principle – never sit at the front in alternative theatre – I thought I was safe, though he was getting closer and louder.

'Conventional theatre,' he barked, 'involves a play-safe contract between actor and audience. Zis contract tonight we break.' Would he spot me? Would it be – 'and you, sir, come out and pretend to be a critic, ja?' I escaped. It wasn't a bad play – simply not one at all.

Late the following afternoon, since I was back in my home city, I decided to revisit Stewart's Hotel, where, since the days of the Pram Factory, the tribe always gathered. Like the Painters and Dockers, the group – writers, actors, publishers, academics – looks after its own and punishes its own. I had left this network, implying that its closeness, its gossip, its affairs were not good enough – and worse, I'd left it for Sydney. Abandoned Melbourne content for Sydney style.

And here, as I got out of the taxi and crossed Elgin Street, was the proof. I was wearing my Gold Coast white pants and hitherto successful pink shirt. It was unseasonably sunny and the drinkers were out on the footpath – and the drinker-in-chief, Dinny O'Hearn, Carlton identity and sub-dean of the Melbourne University Arts Faculty, began jeering at me. A man I'd always got on well with, a praiser of me in the *Age* book pages, now drunk and unshaven, took special exception to my prized shirt – Sydney poof! Paddington parader!

It was a ritual humiliation, during which the others remained silent, and I could only re-establish myself by submitting with good grace. When I was through the gauntlet, a millionaire businessman and writer, in jeans as dirty as Dinny's, brought me out, as a sign of tribal acceptance, the biggest glass of beer I'd ever seen – so big the publican came out after it to make sure it wasn't stolen.

Some weeks later, Billy Marshall, one of my screenwriting students from the Film School, told me that the Aboriginal people of Papunya (he'd spent years teaching there) had institutionalised this kind of mockery into the Teasing Group. The outsider is teased by the group, and this helps bind it together. Their favourite insult, their equivalent to Sydney poof, is directed at ears – because they relate intelligence to hearing. *Pina wima*! *Pina wima*! – Little ears! Little ears! And some say, according to Billy, they tease more when in danger of losing their Dreaming. The Stewart's Hotel tribe were losing some of theirs – the Pram Factory, their sacred site, was now derelict a hundred metres down the road.

My first visit to Brisbane was equally unpromising. The Queensland Theatre Company's adaptation of *Animal Farm*, involving twenty-three actors in animal costumes and a small orchestra, was bad, and their public relations man knew it. He greeted me effusively, took me straight to the bar and kept asking if I'd like another whisky. I kept saying yes. But even five in rapid succession failed to dull my critical sensibilities. The sight of anthropomorphic figures capering to music and doing *Playschool* violence to the original's spare prose was so painful it prevented sleep. The low hum that could be heard between numbers could have been Orwell spinning at turbine speed in his grave.

Because I phoned my copy in, there were typos every week. 'And the baby was suffocated' became 'and the baby was sophisticated'. It could have been worse. When Clive Barnes reviewed *A Midsummer Night's Dream* for the *New York Times*, he wrote that he'd found David Wallace's Bottom particularly splendid, but the crucial word came out in lower case.

By November 1986, after only three months, the paper's circulation is declining, and there have been crisis meetings at Fairfax (would I get the sack? Could they afford me – the interstate flights, the hotels?). Worse, Kristin Williamson tells me Robert Haupt might go. Candy Baker, who's taken over as arts editor (is that the third in as many months?) says the *National Times on Sunday* office is like the Mad Hatter's Tea Party. Later still, as we take the long pathway to the Wharf Theatre to see *Tom and Viv*, Robert Drewe tells us Haupt has just resigned, to be replaced by Valerie Lawson. As we take the same boardwalk after the show, Robert Haupt's in front of us. We have to go slowly so as not to catch up. What could I possibly have said?

There are some theatre experiences that move into the backstage of memory and refuse to leave, and Barry Dickins's *Royboys*, which I was permitted to fly to Melbourne to review, is one of them. It was an elegy to the recently deceased Fitzroy Football Club, and it was staged in the plush depths of the Arts Centre. Amongst the usual crowd there were some very large men – famous footballers, at ease in their native jungle habitat but awkward and uncertain here – such as Jack Dyer, now a little stooped, and the man whose name Dyer, as a radio commentator, was unable to pronounce – Robert Dieperdomenico. (Dyer used to do almost as much damage to the English language as he did to his opponents. A well-known coach, he once noted, had just come back from 'the French Riverina', and a particularly tall ruckman was once described as extending his arms 'like a pair of giant testicles'.)

After I found my seat up the back the whole row started to tremble. A giant was heading for the one next to me. It was Ray Gabelich, huge in his Collingwood playing days and even bigger now. He sits, and my seat sinks into his, and I spend much of the evening leaning against him. But what was going on? Ray can't work it out. Why is this white-haired guy taking notes all the time, like some kind of football coach? And why is he pressing up against me?

Fitzroy, the Royboys, eternal losers, get some goals on the scoreboard at last. Beryl and Roy Noble have stuck with them to the end. Roy is sixty and alcoholic, the old Australia personified, the Australia that's going up the street in a removalist's van. He's battling the pink-helicopter entrepreneur who wants to shift Fitzroy to Tokyo. He fails, collapses and dies, his face falling into a plate of rissoles. ('Don't die yet, love, you haven't done the lawns.')

Roy might lose, but the play's a winner – even Roy's old blue heeler behaves itself. She barks at their quarrels, chases any actor that runs, sniffs the set, and falls through the floor. It's a great night, and Dickins celebrates by kicking a football across the foyer, narrowly missing the Jeffrey Smart murals.

A few weeks earlier, I went over to the other side myself. I'd been commissioned by Angus & Robertson to devise what they called a presentation to celebrate their centenary. It would be at the Opera House, and must be centred around their founder, George Robertson. But – Scottish and thrifty to the end, like Robertson himself – the budget was modest, and costs 'mustn't get out of hand'.

George Robertson, I soon discovered, was the most underrated figure in Australian literature. A Scot, big, bearded and blunt, he was as unsparing of the talentless ('Dear Sir, Your stories are quite hopeless and we feel sure that you will never do anything worthwhile. Give it up and take to gardening, or something else that's useful, in your spare time') as he was nurturing of the gifted. He started his publishing career with a whip crack: Banjo Paterson became the most popular English-language poet of his time (apart from Kipling) and he went on to build an unmatched Australian list – C.J. Dennis, May Gibbs, Norman Lindsay, Christopher Brennan and Henry Lawson, who both delighted him and drove him mad. He had a hiding place at the back of his bookshop to which he retreated whenever Lawson came in, begging for booze money. From 1900 until his death in 1933 he dominated Australian publishing.

It wasn't easy to suggest all this with half-a-dozen actors reading from their scripts, but under Nick Enright's direction they moved backwards and forwards in rhythmic patterns to the music of Elgar. But it was intimate theatre, in constant danger of disappearing into the whale-gape of the Opera House.

It was around this time that I saw Valerie Lawson, now the paper's editor, at the Paddington newsagency, rearranging the disturbingly high stack of *Times on Sunday* in the hope more people would notice it. If it's not selling in Paddington, then where? A few days later, a call from the most recent arts editor. 'This is strictly between you and I. I've just resigned.' (Between you and *I*? That's a sackable offence in itself.)

The paper kept sinking, the deck sloping slightly, but I was allowed to stay on board. I can remember little of the plays reviewed for the rest of 1987. But I still have some of the cuttings, now turning brown. 'Lights up on Jennifer Clare as Lillian Hellman' began one. No recollection of that whatever. 'The situations are slow-paced and unsubtle, the language flavourless basic English.' So much so that the play, *The Impostor* by a Chinese playwright called Sha Yexin, has disappeared entirely.

There's an irony here. When scholars write the theatrical history of the time, the only evidence they'll have to go on will be the reviews. The productions will have submerged, all their lights gradually extinguished, leaving on the surface only a thin slick of type. The reviewers' accounts of the plays become the authorised versions. All that vividness and fire collapsing into the ash blackness of print.

There were vividness and fire in the epic production of Manning Clark's *History of Australia*, a perhaps foolhardy attempt to transform Clark's vast six-volume work into dialogue, dance and song, staged in the faded French–Empire finery of Melbourne's Princess Theatre. The proscenium arch disappeared into a wraparound set that brought gum trees and action into the audience. Eighty-eight characters came and went, taking the audience on a boisterous ride through two centuries of history. Something almost as spectacular followed – a tremendous party in the Melbourne Town Hall, at which Bob Hawke, that legendary theatre-lover and patron of the arts, gave a speech.

Sometimes the play took off, and sometimes it was as chaotic as the period it was depicting. Knowing the time, effort and money the producers, writers, composers and performers had put into it, my review focused on the good – the vigour, the energy – but the Melbourne *Sun* was savage, and the *Age*'s Len Radic, the Easter Island obelisk, was stony. It closed after thirty-seven performances. Later, the journalist Ben Hills pecked away at it like a crow at roadkill, carefully avoiding the central point: Manning Clark's *History of Australia* was a heroic enterprise that deserved admiration, not cheap journalistic contempt.

A month later, it was another heroic enterprise's turn. I wrote a review of a now-forgotten Melbourne Theatre Company play on the forty-second floor of the Regent Hotel, working until 3 am, and watching the lights of the city shrinking far below me. A few hours later, I rang the *Times on Sunday* to file. 'Don't bother,' said my contact, Sharon Hill, who was in tears. 'The paper's folded.' Was it my room service bills that did it?

By May 1988, when I was still luxuriating in the fact that I'd never have to manhandle 800 words out of a brightly lit couple of hours whose meaning eluded language, we began to run out of money. We were still getting free tickets, but – the crucial part of a theatrical experience – couldn't afford interval drinks. 'Don't worry, dear,' said my mother during one of our regular Sunday night phonecalls. 'When one door closes, another opens.' If she suspected I might have been hinting about a short-term loan, she was right.

Her venerable apothegm turned out to be right too. In June, I went to a lunch organised by Geoffrey Dutton for what he called key figures, to meet Christopher Pearson, soon to launch a Sydney equivalent of his successful *Adelaide Review*. Pearson, rotund of figure and orotund of speech, took me aside and offered me one hundred dollars a review for his new monthly. Despite our indigence, I declined. The next day he doubled the offer. 'Please say yes,' he said. Though I was flattered (by the pleading, not the pay) and told him I'd think about it, I knew I'd have to take it on.

But we couldn't live on $200 a month. Carmel keeps us afloat managing a rug shop and writing video scripts for the Education Department. From now on we eke – a verb that sounds better without a predicate. I agree to be strapped once again into theatrical harness and drag 1200 words behind me once a month for Pearson's *Sydney Review*. While I was straining at my task, I got a phonecall from Anne Fussell, features editor of the *Australian*. 'Is it true you're interested in being literary editor of the paper?' (I had my friend Dick Hughes, who worked then at News Limited, to thank for this masterly piece of networking.) Saved! I wanted to shout, but managed a sober affirmative instead.

‘You’re going to be what?’ said my mother, when I phone her with the news. ‘You’ll be the literary? It was my prayers that did it.’ Try as I might, my mother persisted in using literary as a noun.

Frank Devine, soon to become the *Australian*’s editor, rings from New York, sounding more serious than the roaring rollicker I knew from dinner parties. He wants my ideas in a letter straight away. ‘See ya, kid,’ he signed off, with a friendliness that had a slight undertone of menace, which sent me into a depression. I’d failed at film, I’d failed at radio, I’d taken to the lifeboats with a sinking newspaper – could this be the quadrella?

The terror of the machines

About a month later – it’s July 1988 now – I had lunch with Geoffrey Dutton. He was giving up the literary editorship and passing it on to me. We talked books and gossip and then, over the coffee, he asked whether I could use ‘the machines’.

‘The what?’

‘The VDTs.’

‘I’m sorry?’

‘Video Display Terminals.’ No I could not. ‘Don’t panic – if you can type there’ll be no problem.’

But there was a problem. I couldn’t type. I was a longhand man, a vestige, a fossil, and as he took me back to the office I felt afraid. The fear grew when we entered the fluorescent vastness of the newsroom, swelled as we sat down in front of a Video Display Terminal – and, as Dutton’s fingers pecked at the keyboard in accordance with codes I didn’t understand, terror turned to panic.

'Don't worry,' said the good friend who'd helped me get the job. 'I'll teach you at night when there's no one around.' Every night when I arrived for tuition, my friend would insist on going first to the Evening Star for what he called the theoretical work. Five or six beers later we'd go back for the practical side – but his words would go in one ear, float across to the other and out again.

The anxiety and the bottleneck lasted three months, partly because I'd made the job a lot harder. Dutton, with whom I was briefly apprenticed, would go in only two days a week, open drawers by now bulging with books, and assign them at speed, like a dealer with a pack of cards. For him it was a part-time job – he was a writer who did this on the side. When Frank Devine took over as editor, he asked if there was anything I wanted. A third page, I foolishly replied. Done, he boomed.

Three broadsheet pages was a frightening amount of space and it was up to me to fill it. I started a feature called 'Behind the Book', with a writer or publisher interviewed every week, and columns from London, New York (and Sydney). The books arrived in waves – boxes and boxes of them – and I made two discoveries. Even three pages were inadequate (Frank eventually let me increase it to four) and so were a depressing number of reviewers I'd inherited.

'Be ruthless,' said Frank – and there was no other way. The uneditable were never published, and the salvageable rewritten so comprehensively I hoped their authors would be annoyed, and refuse to contribute any further. This disposed of some but not others, and when they got no more books to review and asked why, I had to tell them, using euphemisms like 'a new look' and 'fresh faces'. It fooled nobody. I'd made my first enemies (apart from theatrical ones).

The book review, I now realised, was an art form in itself, and it took months to purge the pages of those who couldn't do it. A handful survived. It sounds easy, but it isn't, and I set out in search for those who might have the gift – extending from academic and literary magazines to letter writers in the broadsheets. There were discoveries – the acerbic Kathy Hunt, Gippsland's Dorothy Parker, a pungent humorist called Greg Flynn who was rapidly terminated by my successor James Hall; and disasters – the most unexpected being a prize-winning novelist whose copy was so bad it was a puzzle how he could have written a novel at all. He expressed himself crisply nevertheless when his review was sent back for a second time – 'Get fucked'.

But the challenge was only beginning. The right book had to be mated with the right reviewer. Out went flesh-coloured novels with embossed titles, airport fiction, cooking, dieting and self-help works, and the bafflingly obscure: *The Romance of Milk: The Story of Australian Dairying*; *Will and Codicil: The Trustee Company Story*; *From Bedpan to Trepan: Post-war Hospital Policy*. (I made all these up, but there were many of this kind.)

Literary editors operate like escort agencies. Matchings need diplomacy (is A a friend or enemy of B? Wasn't C an ex-lover of D? Didn't E once get a bad review from F?)

It didn't take long for the letters and faxes to come in (no emails, mercifully, yet). One outraged author copied the letter he'd sent to the reviewer of his book to me. 'Dear D, I have just seen your review of my book in the *Weekend Australian*. Is this the same D who was a colleague and friend at the ABC? Goodness, what a silly old fart you have become.'

But ultimately it's always my fault. 'Dear Barry, When I was foolish enough to ask you if you were going to review my book, I had no idea you would send it to X. Surely you must have known that X regards Henry Lawson as his personal property, and that trespassers are shown the gate? His review was motivated by spleen from beginning to end, and parts of it may be defamatory. Thanks for your help. We must have a beer sometime.'

An entire eco-system had to be mapped and mastered. As well as disgruntled authors and sacked reviewers, publishers and literary agents also circled, alert for omissions. There being no such thing as a free lunch, if either of the above took me to one, favours were implicitly expected in return. The longer and more expensive the lunch, the greater the implied obligation. A literary editor must be able to hold his or her liquor.

At the system's centre is the heave and bubble of Australian literary pond-life. Who are the carps, who the tadpoles? And what of the few that have made the salmon-leap to international waters, and who will henceforth regard any local criticism as small-pond envy and malice?

There were also literary lunches, arranged in partnership with large department stores, and as a result offering authors one didn't always admire. Like the absurdly popular Ken Follett, whose prose I sample before introducing him to an admiring crowd of North Shore and Eastern Suburbs matrons. I stumbled through his new novel until reaching a sex scene: 'This was not what was supposed to happen, she thought weakly. He pushed her gently backward on the bed, and her hat fell off. This isn't right, she said feebly. He kissed her mouth, nibbling her lips gently with his own.' As a general rule, the more adverbs, the worse the writer. In four sentences, Follett had cobbled in four of them.

At another, I had to introduce Sidney Sheldon, an even more successful writer, before an even larger admiring crowd.

Sheldon's novels are written in sentences like processed cheese, but have sold, according to the press release, 300 million copies (I don't believe it). Some of my incredulity must have shown when I introduced him. As I came down from the podium and he came up, he whispered, 'You took that off the press release.' It was true – I could think of no compliments of my own – but I denied it. He had trouble fixing his features into a smile.

Pretending to enthuse (in my capacity as Literary Editor of the *Australian*) about the processed-cheese prose of US author, Sidney Sheldon.

One must also be alert for the Richler Effect. I admired the novels of the Canadian humorist (*Solomon Gursky Was Here*) and his publishers organised a lunch for him. At the table I was introduced to a small, sour figure who I assumed to be the author's father, but who turned out to be Mordecai Richler, the author himself. The open-faced forty-year-old of his new novel's jacket photo had undergone a Dorian-Gray transformation into someone elderly and sullen. Maybe he was aware of the effect, because he spent most of the lunch turned away from us, puffing on smelly cheroots. And when I later met Joseph Heller, the keen-eyed kibbitzer on the *Good As Gold* flyleaf had metamorphosed into a copper-skinned Gold Coast retiree.

Though the literary editor isn't high in the newsroom pecking order (real journalists see it as a sheltered workshop) I learned to use what little power I had to delegate unpleasant assignments – especially interviewing writers. With rare exceptions (Amos Oz for one) writers are solipsists who believe their work is a nebula at the centre of the universe. (I know – I'm one myself.) The more important they think they are, the harder they play to get. Gore Vidal – the last of the American Puritans, for whom political life is irredeemably corrupted – fortunately said no. Sliding down the significance scale, Murray Bail, who's taken up residence in literature's cold store, also refused. (The literary journalist Michele Field told me that when she was doing a series of writer interviews, Bail would only consent to leave the coolroom if he could be assured he wouldn't encounter any other writer going out or coming in.)

As well as the Richler Effect, another principle soon established itself. The less the talent, the more the self-promotion. A poet sent me a monthly newsletter of his activities, expecting to get an occasional mention in Lyn Tranter's column about local literary life. When she did mention him (critically) I had a call from the offended poet. 'I don't want to threaten you, but steps might have to be taken if something isn't done. She could well affect my chances of getting grants.' 'Threaten away,' I said, and hung up.

His poems didn't get in either. Poetry editorship came with the job, which led to the formulation of a third literary law: the White Mice Syndrome. When our children were young, they had white mice, which, tormented by their confinement, sometimes turned on one another in a flurry of squealing. Poets, maddened by obscurity, can sometimes do the same.

Novelists and playwrights resent their more successful colleagues, but poets coalesce into hostile camps. The modernists and traditionalists hate one another, and on at least one occasion have come to blows.

All over Australia, I soon discovered, bad poetry was being written. Some aspirants couldn't even get my title right: 'The Littery editor', 'The Lisenary editor', 'the overall editor of literature'. Some were so bad a certain majesty crept into them:

> *How is one to loosen up the serious*
> *boondoggle of the species from afar?*

From a Japanese poet ('I enclose some my manuscripts and expect your good answer'):

> *I might was selfish*
> *I might was coward*
> *Please don't forget our life*
> *Teardrops of elephant.*

Even when a poem was published, you weren't safe. 'Dear Barry Oakley, I have been contacted by Mr X, in relation to his poem *Apology to my Father*. I gather from Mr X that there was a misprint in the third verse, and he would like a correction published.' Sincerely, Lynne Spender, Executive Officer, Australian Society of Authors.

Exasperated limpidity

Late in 1989, two things came out – *The Craziplane*, my fourth novel, and my gallstones. While Bert Hingley, the short, dapper and sharp publisher at Hodder & Stoughton, was doing repair work on the manuscript, covering it with Post-it stickers, my doctor, the courtly Meyer Marshall, told me I was going to need some editing too.

I had resumed theatre reviewing, this time with the paper Max Suich had always wanted to publish – *The Independent Monthly*. (I'd abandoned the *Sydney Review* to protect my liver, after Christopher Pearson, increasingly cash-strapped, started paying me with cartons of Petaluma white wine.)

On my way back from Justin Fleming's play *Harold in Italy*, I suffered stitch-like pains, and had trouble walking. Was it post-theatrical dialogue poisoning, or something worse? At Meyer Marshall's insistence, I took the treadmill test at St Vincent's, where Dick Hall lay recuperating from a heart attack – sustained, aptly enough, at a book launch (perhaps after learning he had to pay for his drinks).

The heart was okay. Next came the ultrasound, and when Marshall inspected the results he found them so remarkable he called in his colleague to look. The gallbladder was stuffed like Kerry Packer's wallet with six large stones.

'You should be in agony,' he said, 'and yet all you get are pains while walking.'

I'd now agreed to some – but not all – of Bert Hingley's editorial suggestions, and accepted the cover art (the playwright Frank Minogue, fat and fluorescent, flying over night-time Carlton). Would the book come out before the bladder?

No. My wife sent me to Grace Brothers for hospital

pyjamas, and I met James Murray, the *Australian*'s Religious Affairs writer. 'Oh,' he said, when I told him why I was there. 'My father had to have his gallbladder out, and he bled to death on the operating table.' I thanked him for his Christian consolation. Rose Cresswell too had encouraging words. 'Don't worry, you'll have intense pain for three days, and then you'll pick up.'

At the hospital, I'm told to wait until 4 pm. There were nine hours to fill in. I had secreted a valium – forbidden before surgery – and now took it. Eventually I was trolleyed in, the men in green masks loomed over me, and I lost consciousness. Rose Cresswell was right. There was serious pain afterwards, especially when I coughed or laughed. On these rare occasions I pressed a pillow against my gut. The incision looked enormous. I was stitched up like a sherrin.

The Craziplane came out a month later, launched by Peter Carey in the upper room of the Bellevue Hotel, in Paddington. How slim it looked, compared to the fatness of his *Illywhacker*! It's an ideal place for a launch – there's a bar, and there's only one entrance, which makes it hard for freeloaders to slip away without buying the book. The furtive departure of two old friends was duly noted.

I'll be brief. *The Craziplane* is the story of Frank Minogue, Australia's greatest living playwright, his actress wife, and Michael, an aspiring writer who's attempting Frank's biography (fails) and an affair with his wife (succeeds).

Had my book, I asked in my thank you speech, had a hospital experience similar to my own? Bert Hingley had been handed a meaty 220 pages, only for it to come out at a malnourished 141. Like me, it went in as rump steak and came out a diet biscuit. Even an epigraph would have helped by adding a page, and too late, I had one ready, taken from a bottle of Lambrusco recently consumed. 'If you are expecting an exasperated limpidity, you will not be disappointed.'

The reviews were good ('may well be the most delightful Australian novel to appear this year' – Judith White, Sydney *Sun Herald*) with one exception. I'd left the job of finding a reviewer for the pages I edited to Frank Devine, and he chose a splenetic New Zealander who took exception to the sex scenes and was generally not amused. Strange to read a critical review of one's own book in one's own pages.

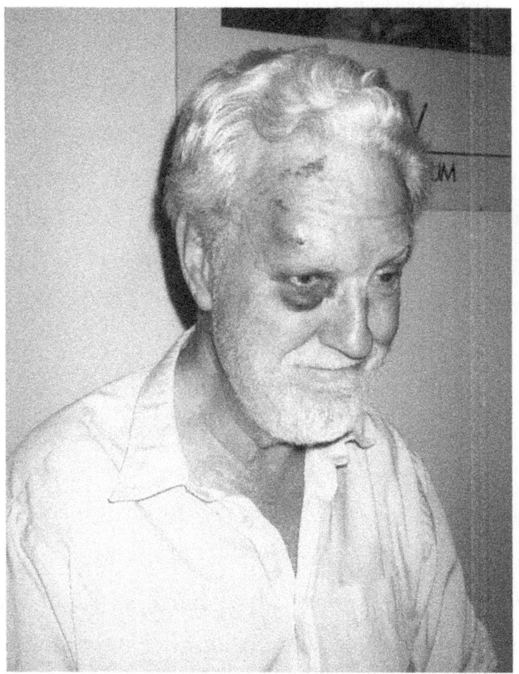

Slight mishap after Frank Devine's farewell lunch.

Slow fade

It was hard to get details of my father's illness because he and my mother rarely spoke. It had been thus for forty-five years. Their exchanges over all that time generally consisted of 'your tomatoes are ready' (breakfast) and 'your dinner's in the oven' (dried to a crisp by the time he came home).

It was only when I made my regular Sunday phonecall to my mother that I learned my father had gone into St Vincent's hospital the previous Tuesday. He had survived an aneurism operation, the surgeon told me, and must have had an iron constitution to have done so.

When I managed to get through to him he sounded weak and said he didn't want to keep going. He had developed pneumonia, and I flew down to Melbourne immediately. Had they moved him up to the ninth floor to die? He looked frail and exhausted, but unnervingly alert. He stared at me in a way he'd never done before (we'd never been close). It made me feel uncomfortable, and I looked away. 'I've always taken the easy way out,' he said, referring to our unusual domestic arrangements.

Then I took the easy way out and changed the subject. I had the feeling my father wanted to talk to me about the double life we knew he'd led for so many years, and I didn't want to hear it. So I asked him about *his* father, who'd founded the estate agency. He said he'd worked him hard, and sent him round South Yarra on a bike collecting rents. I have no memory of him. He died in the early 1930s. His photograph rested on the mantelpiece in our house in Montague Avenue. He was walking along St Kilda pier, and looked as if he'd stepped out of John Brack's painting *Collins St., 5 pm*: the hat, the glasses, the grimness.

A fortnight later I returned to Melbourne to see my father again. He'd wasted away even more. There seemed only two dimensions to him. I hold his hand. It's withered and browned, like an autumn leaf. A diminutive, determined-looking woman comes in who I first took to be a nurse's aide. Then I realise it's Beryl, whom I'd last seen walking rapidly down our drive in 1944, carrying a cheap brown suitcase. My mother had ordered her out of the house. We exchange polite greetings, then, tactfully, she leaves.

A week afterward I'm in St Vincent's as well, the Sydney one, being wheeled into the operating theatre. I'd been referred to a Dr Carter, an orthopaedic surgeon – silver hair, face like a baked apple – about my right arm, which had been stiff and sore for months. He'd moved it up and down, had me raise it as high as possible as if Hitler had been in the room.

'Frozen shoulder,' he snaps.

'Will it have to come off?' I attempted, knowing he was grumpy and terse. He stared at me, puzzled (are there laughing, joking orthopaedic surgeons?). He was a heavy breather, and in need of an adenoid man himself.

'Sign yourself in for a day in hospital on the way out.'

So I was trolleyed in (again) and noticing the silver hair above the surgeon's mask (was he smiling? looking forward to revenge?) I was unable to avoid irritating him again. 'It's the right one, remember?' and then I passed out, after which the frozen arm was turned into a propeller, giving off loud pops as the glued tendons gave way. I woke up in agony, and it took weeks of numbingly tedious physiotherapy before I could manage a full Nazi salute.

While I was complaining of post-operative shoulder pain, my father was dying. I rang each day, and his voice became weaker and weaker, until he slurred that he couldn't hear me, and he died the next day, 24 February 1990, my birthday.

On the following Wednesday our family walked along the same path behind the Christian Brothers' residence that my father had dragged me down screaming fifty-two years earlier to begin my schooldays at CBC St Kilda. We took the front pews of St Mary's church, where I'd been confirmed by Archibshop Mannix, and where Carmel and I had married. Our mother is on my right, with my brother on her other side. She's looped with pearl necklaces, which give out a faint clink as she looks around, to see what the enemy is up to. One of my brother's daughters is letting her down. (Loudly) 'Naomi is talking to Beryl.'

Our mother's upset because, the day after the family death notices were published, there appeared, in the same papers, the following: 'Oakley, Harry. Thank you for the love we shared. Poppy.'

Though my father had swapped Catholicism for the Masons many years before (and had once horrified me as a schoolboy by lighting a cigarette in St Patrick's Cathedral), he had been received back into the Church in his last moments. As our mother had commented: 'Your father's always been late for everything.' During the Requiem Mass, one image kept coming back to me – the dash he had once made from a Sorrento hotel to the gangway of the paddle-steamer *Weeroona* on one of its pre-war bay cruises. Though I would have been six at the time, it was still vivid – the ship's whistle, the engine's rumble, the crew releasing the mooring ropes, and the cheers of his estate-agent friends as he just made it aboard. Had he done the same with eternal life?

'I am the resurrection and the life,' intoned the priest, portly, empurpled. 'If anyone believes in me, even though he dies, he will live.' I had the feeling that our father, trapped, lying only a few metres away, as he had done on an eternity of Sunday afternoons, was listening, possibly with gritted teeth.

Struggling up the rope ladder

By now I too had climbed aboard again. After the birth of our sixth child Kieran in 1970, rather than spend the rest of our married lives worrying about the discordancies of the rhythm method, we had left the Catholic Church.

But I felt directionless without it. When John Paul II came to Sydney in 1986, and said Mass at Randwick Racecourse before a huge crowd, I watched it on TV. Though in those days he was still vigorous, his address wasn't promising. 'Tank you for your kind vords and locutions.' But then, wisely, he abandoned his notes, extended his arms, and said 'Kahm Bach! Kahm Bach!' pleading for the lapsed to return. I was moved – he seemed to be talking to me – even more so when he walked over to the crowd: love made visible.

From that time I followed at a safe distance, like Peter and the arrested Christ. When the priest said the words quoted above at my father's Mass, a barrier collapsed, and I did believe that my father still lived (albeit in some transcendental version of his favourite haunt, the South Yarra Club).

And the Church I was now reluctantly approaching had travelled a distance itself. What was once called confession was now reconciliation, done in daylight, face to face with the priest. Fortunately, Sydney's St Mary's Cathedral still catered for cowards. One could confess there in the old anonymous dimness of the box with the sliding panel.

So one day I lined up with the other sinners, waited my turn, warned the priest that it was a long time since my last confession and unloaded twenty years of culpabilities onto his bald, bowed head. He took it calmly, made the absolving sign of the cross, gave me an undemanding penance, and I went out blinking into the light.

The real transformation came later, at the Easter Sunday Mass. The quiet nudgings that had urged me on now pushed me to the altar rails, to receive a pale circle of unleavened bread that at the consecration becomes, impossibly, the body of Christ. It feels uncomfortable to talk about this mystery – it's private, in the way married love is private – but after one has taken the Host there's a stillness: being (ours) invaded by Being; love (our meagre portion) by Love. It's food, and it's the secret life of the Catholic Church: lifeblood pulsing up from the parishes, not down from Rome. You receive a great gift, and when you take the gift, you taste the giver.

How can one believe it? How can one believe we're heading for fullness and not nothingness, a state of purer being, a spirit-marriage with God? I did then and I do now, to the bemusement of our children and the mockery of friends. 'Faith without works is dead,' said St Paul. But faith *is* a work. Sometimes it carries you, and sometimes, in the face of derision and incredulity, you carry it.

Cripple kicked

Literary editorship might have been a sheltered workshop, but the lathes and pulleys never stopped whirring, and one had to be careful not to get caught in them. Frank Devine, to whom I'd been close, was replaced by David Armstrong, to whom I wasn't. Sometimes, when editors are replaced, section editors can go too. One morning, as I huddled into my primitive, hooded VDT hunting and pecking – was keyboard ineptitude a ground for dismissal? – I noticed Armstrong coming down our way from the executive end.

I huddled lower, but he was heading not for me but a neighbour, a sub-editor I'll call B. B was a gay, civilised but troubled man, whose breath smelt of alcohol when he arrived of a morning. B was ushered into an empty office, told how much the editor regretted having to do this, handed an envelope, and sacked. B came out stunned, his normally florid complexion as white as the envelope he was holding. 'I've just been sacked,' he said to me. 'On the spot. Just like that. His hand was shaking when he handed me the envelope.'

I walked up to the staffroom for a steadying coffee, while B collected his things. M, the travel editor, a grim, unsmiling man, looked equally stunned. 'I've just been sacked. How'd you like a trip to India?' I accepted – though was it wise to turn one's back right now? Should I check to see if my job was safe? No – lie low in the hope one won't be noticed, like Mike Wellington, the drama critic in Howard Brenton's and David Hare's play *Pravda*, who escapes sacking by the carnivorous new proprietor because he lies drunk under the desk.

So I pressed on and worked hard, repelling boarders before they could get a grip on the rails. There was the man who rang to ask whether I could organise a review of a book he had just self-published – and would I also mind sending him a clipping of the review as he did not take the paper. There was Edwin Morrisby, whose voice locked onto you the moment you answered the phone, the words unspooling from somewhere deep in his head, relentless and uninterruptible, about a feature review he would like to do on medieval Bohemian glass. There was Bob Brissenden, a kind of friend, who insisted on seeing me. I feared the worst. Could there be an interview, when his crime novel came out? Could Geoffrey Dutton, his friend, review his book of poems? And could he, Bob, review the new Scott Turow? All this over a coffee, with Bob bent double under a huge hump, his hands shaking as he probes his wallet – 'I'll pay, I'll pay' – for the change. There was Sandy Yarwood, whose review I rejected, and when he rang to complain couldn't speak properly. 'I've had a stroke,' he managed, and made me feel as if I were kicking a cripple. India, quickly!

Optical enjoyment

When I leave the plane at what was then called Madras, one of a small group of freeloading journalists, the heat, noise, and smells coalesce into a single overpowering entity, like a slap in the face. It's nearly midnight, but the airport's packed. It heaves, it babbles – especially the porters, who fight over our luggage, lead us ceremoniously to our taxis, and await our tip – the first of many.

We bump and honk into town along a road lined with people, stalls and shacks, the air heavy with cooking and sewage smells. Even at midnight, all India seems to be moving – medieval trucks, bullock wagons, impossibly overloaded handcarts, teetering motor scooters, cows – a river, a procession, a parade.

It's still going when I pull back the hotel drapes early next morning. When we join the flow in our minibus and visit a Hindu temple, the pressure seems to force its way through the entrance and push upwards, forming tier after tier of writhing figures. Gods by the hundred, rising up into the crow-circled sky.

There's life in Indian silences as well as sounds. We take the coast road to Mamallapuram, once the great port of the Pallava dynasty, then mysteriously abandoned. Huge granite sculptures are all that's left, rising up from the sand, with dim figures rippling along their sides. A wind from the sea blows around them. It seems to whisper in a language I'll never understand. As we leave, we pass a group of squatting women. One of them opens her basket, revealing a cobra. It's tired and old, and has to be cuffed before it will rear up. Then she produces an equally elderly mongoose in a tiny leather harness. 'Photo? You want photo?'

We leave the state of Tamil Nadu to move on to Karnataka, whose capital is Bangalore (soon to become the centre of the Indian IT industry). Our guide takes us on a walk through the city (Panama Cigarettes – Good to the Last Puff, Ding Dong Ice Cream, Dr Cleatus: Diseases of the Bone) and we spend the evening in a Bangalore bar (Liquor Ruins Country, Family and Life).

Just before we leave the town, a magician performs in the shade by the side of our minibus. He wears a silver turban and a vest of silver and blue squares. He takes a deep breath, exhales fire and smoke, then disgorges batch after batch of nails. When he smiles, there's a hole where his teeth should be. All that firing and smoking have turned his mouth into an exhaust pipe.

Near Mysore, the landscape changes. Dryness gives way to rice paddies and greenness. This is the India we expected, and we stop so it can be photographed. One of the watching children scoops up water from the paddy field and drinks. 'You must never do that,' our guide warns us. 'They develop a resistance. You do it, and you are within forty-eight hours dead.'

The Maharajah's palace ('Please leave your shoes here only and enter one by one') at Mysore is vast and vulgar, a Luna Park of domes, its endless marzipan corridors lined with portraits of past dignitaries, plump and glossy and rich. As we emerge, a beggar sees us coming and lies back to show off the stumps of his legs. The gap between the palatial and the impoverished seems unbridgeable, predetermined.

Our cross-country journey ends at Cochin, on the west coast – the Malabar Coast, centre of the old spice trade. From my hotel window there's an unforgettable view over the lagoon: high-prowed fishing boats chugging out to the Arabian Sea, rusty freighters coming in, overcrowded rowing boats propelled by a single straining oarsman, Edwardian ferries. In the distance, at the port's entrance, you can see the high spidery frames of the Chinese fishing nets, and from across the water come the wails of the *muezzin*. Vasco de Gama's grave is here, and down a mustard-coloured laneway there's a tiny synagogue, 400 years old.

The hotel brochure puts it well: 'A walk down to the port composes optical enjoyment. We recommend your walk there with full moon.' After doing so, in our last South Indian twilight, heavy with the smell of Aerogard and make-up, we watch the *kathakali*, the classical dance of Kerala, in which Shiva, magnificent in black, gives the sacred arrow to Arjuna, robed in red. Cochin is as layered in history as the two young actors are in paint and silks: Hindu, Chinese, Portuguese, Jewish, Muslim.

For me, the symbol of India was a concrete building with steel reinforcing rods sprouting from the roof. No one has bothered to round it off. The finished look was not important. Everything, in the Hindu view of things, is in a state of becoming. We must live our worldly lives with an eye to *mokṣha*, release. The street and shops might decay, but for the holy person the outer world can't gain entry to the inner one. In the heart of the squalor lives a spiritual idea, which is why the memory of India refuses to go away.

Be prepared

Back in the sublunary world, the cabinets are bulging with books, there's a leaning tower of mail, and twenty-six voicemail messages. One is from Bob Brissenden, thanking me for the interview I'd organised in the previous Saturday's paper. A later one tells me that Bob has just died.

One of literary editorship's greatest trials is the unexpected death. Suddenly the workshop shelter is ripped off, and thirty or forty paragraphs, depending on the importance of the deceased, are required at once. It happened to me with Patrick White (my own fault. I should have had something ready). I was at a party at the time, frantic calls went unanswered, and the following morning's headline read: Poet, Playwright and Novelist Dies. I tried to repair the damage the next day but it was too late.

It happened to me with the Melbourne poet and critic Vincent Buckley. I'd returned from a function to a chilling phone message: sixty-three-year-old Buckley had died, and twenty pars were needed in the next two hours. I managed it, but something went wrong in the production process, and he was turned into an octogenarian: 87-year-old Poet Dies.

It happened to me with Manning Clark. Late in May 1992 the night editor rang. The eminent historian had just died, and could I come in immediately and write something to catch the second edition. I raced to my books, scrabbled through manila folders, and taxied in. At 10.30 pm I was at my desk: 800 words, and forty-five minutes. I managed 500, ran out of gas, flipped through my files, found a piece by the polymathic Peter Craven that I'd rejected, and liposectioned some of its paragraphs while the giant presses in the basement hummed in neutral, waiting, and produced a piece of pure cobbledom, a bricolage of dust-cover blurbs, press cuttings and plagiarism, tapped out with one frantic finger, and none of it telling the truth: Manning Clark was a historian who didn't let the facts interfere with his theories, a poseur in an absurd high hat. A great dramatiser not only of history, but also of himself.

Dusted and dignified

In the same month of the same year, my brother and I had persuaded our mother, now a widow, to move from the family home to a unit in the respectable outer Melbourne suburb of Blackburn. On the morning of the auction, we paid 4 Montague Avenue, East St Kilda, a farewell visit.

The place had been stripped of everything except memories, which seemed to shimmer, along wavelengths beyond the human ear. The old oak bookcase and grandfather clock had gone from the lobby, the bedrooms were bare, and we came to

Brother and self lament the sale of 4 Montague Avenue.

rest in the lounge, my mother's pride, used only on rare occasions when we entertained – when Uncle Tom and Auntie Dot came to play solo, or when Uncle Pat returned from the war, and my father sang his favourite song – 'I'm Forever Blowing Bubbles'. He waved a beer bottle in tune with the music with such vigor he dislodged the lampshade, which bounced on the carpet without breaking.

Normally this was a quiet, dusted and dignified room, with rosewood cabinet and table, dominated by the portrait Rupert Bunny had done of my mother – when my father was away on wartime Thursday Island. She had done the rent collecting, including Bunny's who, then an old man, had a studio in Toorak Road. All these treasures now kept her company in Blackburn.

I used to like the silence and spaciousness of this room, and would sometimes immerse myself in it and gaze up at the stained-glass window (a feature of Californian bungalows of the 1920s) showing an English cottage set in green glass hills with creamy white cloud behind it – a folk memory of Home.

The three of us – mother, brother and I – stood silent in the big bare room, and then she pointed her walking stick at the fireplace. The brass plaque that sat in the grate was still there, covered in dust. I picked it up and rubbed it like Aladdin's lamp, and the bunch of Elizabethan roisterers slowly emerged – first their heads, the table, then the dog at their feet. My childhood seemed to be hidden in that tavern with them, and the more I rubbed the more it came to life.

By noon a crowd was gathering – it seemed indecent in so quiet a street – described as 'leafy' on the auction board. We joined them. The auctioneer, young and smartly suited, stood in the driveway entrance, at the exact spot where my brother would turn, run and bowl at me, Ray Lindwall style, while I did my best to bat like Keith Miller. 'Remember when I lofted an on-drive and cracked one of the top panels of the bow window?' No, my brother didn't. We walked along the driveway and looked up to check – the crack was still there.

There was a worrying silence when bids were first invited, then another when they came to a stop at $190,000. Offers of $5000 were then suggested, then half that, then finally single thousands, which inched the price up to $202,000. Four Montague Avenue was sold to what my mother described as a lovely young couple. We were giving up ownership, but were going to be tenants there always.

Blandness strikes back

It was unusual for James Hall, editor of the *Australian* magazine, to invite anyone to lunch. He spent money as if it were his own and not Rupert Murdoch's (he had accepted a story idea from my friend Luke Slattery, but suggested he take the bus down to Melbourne to do it).

'You're probably wondering why I've invited you to lunch,' he said, as we began on our first (and only) bottle. I had enough tact not to reply. 'I'm not happy with Mungo McCallum's column in the magazine and wondered whether you'd like to take his place. (This would explain why, at an airport years later, when I went up to McCallum, who was dressed in khaki adventurer's outfit and bush hat, looking like an attenuated Ludwig Leichhardt, he dealt me a fleering snub.)

I said I'd think it over, but since McEvoy of the trembling hand had raised the rent again, I had nothing to think over. As the meal progressed and a failed suggestion was made about a second bottle, each of us sank into gloom. Jim said he came from Lincolnshire, the most boring county in England, and feared that some of its forbiddingness had crept into him. 'Not at all,' I lied. Not to be put off, he said he'd been a failure in journalism.

'You edited the *Australian* once.'

'Exactly.' We were getting nowhere, and I was following him down. Eight hundred words a week for months, maybe years: a soapbox that at first might be enjoyable to mount, but which would eventually mount me.

'Another bottle?'

'Only makes me depressed.'

'There you go.' And we did go.

By August, three months in, I'd become something of a whinger, complaining, as I paced my 800-word cage, of the sunny blandness of Australian life. Then the blandness struck back. I was peeling potatoes one Friday evening when there was a frantic banging on the front door – a breathless woman, telling me one of the terraces was on fire. I ran out – the upper storey of the one two doors down from ours was ablaze – then rang the fire brigade.

Ugo, our next-door neighbour, had just done the same. Then we went outside and waited. The fire was already spreading from number twenty to the roof of Ugo's, number twenty-two. He rushed in with Eugene, one of our sons, and saved his computer, as embers fell on their heads. And I went into twenty-four, to save – what? My brain had turned into playdough. Credit cards, cheque books and, as the upper room started to fill with smoke, the cat – tossed out of the back window onto the skillion roof.

Then back to the street. The fire was chewing up the rafters of twenty-two on its way to twenty-four, and the brigade still hadn't arrived. Great smoke swirls sailed into the darkness, more and more people gathered, and one of them said, 'The whole row's going to go up.' I thought of our books, our beds, our clothes, everything that made us what we were, and felt as if I were dying – pictures, papers, possessions, all the layers that grow around the self, about to go. I prayed hard and deep, as I'm sure I'll do when the real thing comes.

The fire engine arrived, but there were more agonising minutes while they tried to find the hydrant. By the time they got the ladder up they'd found the water (it was under the truck) and starting hosing. As in horror movies, the monster took hit after hit and kept on going. I didn't know it then, but there was a firewall between twenty-two and twenty-four. The creature was chomping its way round the wall when it died, exhaling billows of smoke. Our place had taken smoke and water damage, but was saved. Twenty and twenty-two were gone. Carmel, now back from Melbourne, stared at their charred remnants in disbelief. I'd never write of middle-class blandness again.

Part of our roof needed fixing, and was covered by a tarpaulin that leaked when it rained. It was nothing compared to our neighbours' losses, but water came down on our books. I contacted the roofing company and asked if they could hurry up. Yes, we'll do it soon. When was soon? When we can. We waited weeks, the water dripped, I rang again, yes, yes, soon, they were busy with the other terraces. I put a note under one of the windscreen wipers. I'm a columnist. Get it done or I'll do a piece on you.

For the first time, they moved fast. They contacted James Hall, and he gave me a lecture. This was something a columnist never did, and he might have to talk to the editor about it. 'Go ahead, make my day – report me to the headmaster,' I said. I didn't like his tone, and he didn't like mine.

Would I get the sack? From the column? The job? Jim was grim, and demoted me from the front of the magazine to the back. There were more lectures – not too much reminiscence, don't centre it on Sydney, avoid talking about literature. I nodded in assent, and ignored them all.

The uneasy armistice went on. I was starting to run out of ideas. My column had eaten its way through everything I could think of, and was still ravenous for more. I filed when I had ideas, and I filed when I hadn't. I realised that's what all regular columnists do, and I could tell when they did it.

I marvelled at Paddy McGuinness, who, in his prime or nadir, filed 800 fulminating words five days a week – knocked them off in the morning, and then, bloated with opinionation, waddled off to lunch. (He ended his days, a crimson face in an aureole of white hair, holding court to the last remnants of his audience in the Unity Hall Hotel in Balmain.)

I marvelled at how some columnists fill their space with banalities week after week and manage to escape not just the sack but imprisonment for crimes against incisiveness and style. How one of them could escape punishment for beginning a piece like this: 'The other night I sent back my wine. Although we were at a top restaurant, there was a fly in my drink. Such things happen. But the very next day, I had a terrible experience. Drinking my morning coffee at my favourite cafe, I felt something furry in my mouth and spat the coffee everywhere. It was a blow fly. The waiter couldn't believe it had happened twice. "It's too much of a coincidence," he laughed.'

Fearful of such a fate, I spent weekends reading and worrying, or simply hoping that something describable might happen. I got a lively column about the fire, but it was a flood that would give me more. We had rising damp at the front of the house, and, after heavy rain, an inundation at the back. The laundry, which had provided spartan accommodation for Melbourne visitors (John Timlin, Barry Dickins, Clare Forbes, Lucy Frost, Meredith Michie, Margie and Rai Gaita, Patsy and Laurie Clancy, Faith Richmond and Tim Robertson, and from South Australia Jeanne and Brian Matthews) was one night overwhelmed and our house guest at the time awoke to find her bedtime reading floating on the floor. It was time for home ownership.

Finding a house

My late estate agent father had never tired of telling us the rent we'd been paying for years was 'dead money' – and for a tenement at that. It was either buy now or never buy at all.

Our search provided solid column provender for weeks. One Saturday I did some preliminary foraging, hoping, with our modest capital and an equally modest loan, we could still enjoy the pleasures of Paddington. I started with Enchantment Personified: 'The sweetest of terrace houses. Behind a pristine facade, romantic drawing and dining rooms await.' They're still awaiting – the agent said he was looking at the high twos.

I declined to A Place to Hang Your Heart. It was a corner building divided into two dwellings the size and shape of a double-decker bus, with a bathroom so low you'd have to crouch to shower. 'We're looking at ones,' said the saleslady, and looking was all I did.

I finished with a 'one-bedroom hideaway with truly unique three-level layout'. It wasn't so much a terrace as a stage set, behind which you could do no more than get into costume and slip onto the street. There was a bonsai living room, and an upstairs ledge where a ladder led to a stunted attic, where Melbourne visitors (I fantasised) could be sent to deter them from staying again. 'Ones!' shouted the salesman as I exited stage left. 'Low ones!'

We only had enough for a house in the country. A weekender that we'd live in all week. We inspected semi-rural properties bearing no resemblance whatever to the copy that described them. This came to a head with 'Unique Heritage Cottage in the Heart of Windsor. Potential to run a business. $100,000'.

It was a hot day, our car was playing up, and irritation at the weeks of searching bubbled up like a fumarole. 'Heritage' meant run-down, and 'cottage', rooms in which cats could not be swung. And the agent, large-bellied and crimson, kept calling me 'mate'.

Agent: You could run a nice little earner here. Devonshire teas, mate. Handicrafts. Pottery.

Self to wife: And you could do the scones in the galley.

Agent: The galley, mate?

Self: Are you calling that cubicle a kitchen?

Agent (changing tack): You could renovate the shed.

Self: I don't do renovations.

Agent (to wife): Once you get him out here in the country, he wouldn't be so uptight.

Self: I hate the country. We're looking at the country because we can't afford the city.

Wife: That's nonsense.

Self (having meltdown): Do you think my wife's going to bake scones in that lean-to and I'm going to put on a smile and an apron and serve them up to tourists?

Wife (leaving): Sorry about this. Is that an aviary down the back?

Agent (in a sympathetic half whisper to wife): You could keep him in there, love. Enjoy your retirement.

After months wandering the periphery of Sydney, the Blue Mountains were firming. It was looking like Bullaburra, at the bottom of the social scale – then we chanced upon a cottage, four rooms and a shabby bathroom – at Wentworth Falls, that had come on to the market that very day, and which we could almost afford, with a small loan from one of our daughters and a late run on a credit card. Our offer was accepted. After a building inspection ('Ceiling space no leaks in evidence. Mice droppings and one dead mouse present') legalities were formalised, and on 8 October 1996 around 2 pm, I imagine a faint ripple of air in a Wentworth Falls real-estate office – an imperceptible transfer of ownership from the vendor to us. Propertied at last.

Caryatid no longer

A couple of months later, before we'd made the move to the mountains, James Hall hurried into my little office as I hunted and pecked, knelt by my side and told me 'it might be best if your column finished up after another four weeks'. He was agitated, and his voice had a tremble in it. 'Calm down, Jim,' I said. 'I don't mind.' (And though we'd miss the extra money, after four-and-a-half years of searches for a subject, I didn't mind.) The cartoonist Bill Leak, whose studio was next door, came in as soon as James left. 'What's going on? Are you sacking him or is he sacking you?' I told Bill I'd enjoyed it more than James had. That afternoon, as I left the building, I felt like a racehorse whose saddlebags had been unleaded. I could have sprinted home.

I suspected James was acting under instructions. I'd had a run-in with the then editor, who'd had a critical review of one of his books on politics removed from the pages at the last minute without bothering to consult me. I'd then written a memo to him (always get it in writing) to the effect that in pulling the review, he'd put his own interest before that of the reader, and I took strong exception to it.

On my way to drop it into his office, I showed the memo to

the chief sub-editor (always protect your back), which ensured rapid circulation of its contents round the newsroom. The editor was in Canberra, but his deputy, who also got a copy, rang and abused me, and I abused her back. The story leapt across to the rival *Sydney Morning Herald*, where it got an airing. This was bad news for the editor but good for me – it made it hard for him to sack me. But – to use a cliché this same editor was fond of applying to politicians – my days were numbered.

Earlier in my career, John Alexander, then editor-in-chief of the *Sydney Morning Herald*, had offered me a similar job with his paper. When he'd asked my current salary, he'd whistled, and called it 'derisory'. He'd pay me a lot more, but that came with a proviso – he was, he said, very much a hands-on man. Thanks, but no thanks.

Years later (1996 by now) my salary remained derisory, but the editor I'd crossed refused to increase it, maybe hoping to starve me out. When this failed, he announced, like a sentencing magistrate, he'd give me six months. But he went instead, sideways, and his successor gave me another twelve – why not? I was probably the cheapest literary editor in the country.

Misquoted – twice

So I was still there in February 1997, when we moved to Wentworth Falls. After nineteen years of dead money, there were many goodbyes – to Geoffrey Plant, the Franciscan who preached so powerfully at our local church; to the film-making Marriotis, who'd lost almost everything in the fire; to my barber who, during a final cut had said to another customer entering his crowded salon 'No go, mate. Try the wog around the corner', and to Andre, my literary dentist, with whom I'd had one-sided conversations for years. On my farewell visit, he told me he'd just discovered Annie Proulx. Fine, I said, before being gagged with cotton wool, but please check my bridge. Andre was not to be put off. He had the page and the sentence ready: 'At night on the ploughed prairie the darkness was thrown into deeper ink by the sprays of stars, asteroids, comets and planets trembling above him as though in a sidereal wind.' He shook his head. He was miles away.

'The bridge!' I gargled.

'Sidereal wind. I love that.' I pointed at the bridgework, he came to his senses, and probed. 'It could go at any time,' he announced. Only one pylon supported it. So what should I do?

'Don't bite hard.' Condemned to soft food indefinitely, I said goodbye to Andre. 'I'll miss our little talks,' he said. But he was off too. Like so many dentists, he was going to start a vineyard.

Examples from my father's repertoire of axioms have been cited before, and there was another which we unwisely ignored – 'Never accept the lowest quote'. We did, twice.

First with Wally, the Lebanese removalist, who turned up early one morning in a van covered in graffiti. Though he'd checked what had to be moved a few days earlier, now he wasn't sure he could fit it all in. After volleys of obscenities he (a big man) and his assistant (a stripling) got everything out of the house and most of it in the van – but not all. A wardrobe, a chest of drawers and an antique table remained on the footpath.

'We'll have to repack,' Wally said. 'Tight fit. Fucking tight fit. Might cost you a little more.'

'How much more?'

'Maybe fifty.'

We were trapped. Wally repacked, but his silent and largely toothless assistant didn't look well. He'd gone from scarlet from lifting to deathly pale. While Carmel drove on ahead with bits and pieces, the three of us squeezed into the truck cabin. As we groaned towards the mountains Wally attempted banter – 'Poofs on the march tonight. Mardi fucking Gras' – but I was annoyed and didn't respond, while the stripling kept leaning over as if about to faint, and then appeared to fall asleep. 'Fucking weakling,' said Wally, who whistled to fill the silences.

When we arrived, and squeezed our things into the four rooms, Wally had another go. I paid him the extra fifty dollars, but his huge hand was still out.

'Tip?'

'No tip.'

'Let's get out of here,' he said to his bent-over assistant, giving him a whack on the back which almost felled him. Then he slammed the van door and roared off, swearing and shaking his head.

Before we'd moved in we'd had the flooring replaced, but as we moved our furniture around, the cypress pine bounced. The cheap carpenter we'd used had boasted he'd install it with 'invisible nailing', and he was right. He also put in three French doors, but they were so crudely fitted they couldn't be locked, and we spent our first few weeks feeling vulnerable. We'd brought our inner-city wariness with us, and an axe-handle was kept by the bed. But Wentworth Falls was peacefulness itself, though we ended up paying double to keep it that way.

An experienced friend had one piece of advice: have one big room to winter in. He was right. In the Blue Mountains, winter turns from a noun into a verb, and we needed a space to spend it in. My wife, who sometimes has visions rivalling those of Renaissance popes, designed an enormous room. To help pay for it, I stayed on as the *Australian*'s literary editor for ten more months, which involved four-hour round train trips every day. I finished at the end of 1997, after ten years on the job.

The late Frank Devine, by then a columnist at large (in both senses) would sometimes say, loudly and embarrassingly, especially after lunch, that I was the best literary editor the paper had ever had (competence at last!). Bruce Bennett, in the *Oxford Literary History of Australia*, was just as kind: 'The book review section of the *Weekend Australian* became a necessary reference point for opinion and judgement, especially during Barry Oakley's editorship from 1988 until 1997.'

I was given a roaring send-off by my friends and colleagues (with the editor and his deputy absent), staved off genteel poverty with a one-year literary grant, wrote a novel (*Don't Leave Me*), edited my diaries (*Minitudes*) and slipped soundlessly into my seventies.

Old bones

By now I had a new doctor, who'd been told by my old Sydney one that I 'presented unusually', and soon I had a challenge for him. Over the vice-like Blue Mountains winter, I developed a deep ache in the hips that came on at dawn. He pressed and tapped and told me that it wasn't arthritis, as I'd thought. Then he sent me off for X-rays.

Before I took the images back to him I broke the seal on the envelope (To be opened by referring doctor only). Here, like a *Penthouse* feature, was my pelvis from every angle – the skeletal self, mysterious and profound, a coral garden. The accompanying report was in code. There was 'no significant scoliosis or rotational deformity, the vertebral alignment was well maintained'; on the other hand, 'there is mild schmorl's node development in the end-plate surfaces, and minor anterior spondylosis deformans at all levels'. It sounded like what Quasimodo had in *The Hunchback of Notre Dame*. My doctor read it and said that my reputation for bizarre presentation was intact. He sent me to a neurologist.

The neurologist ran over my legs with brushes, pricked my legs with pins, pressed vibrating rods against my ankles, said he was baffled, and sent me off for blood tests. While I was waiting, there was a heavy thump from the other side of the door. Had someone fainted while giving blood? (I was quite capable of it myself.) A Chinese lady came out and I went in. I took off my jacket, but there was no hook to hang it on. The pathologist told me why. When the lady had tried to hang her handbag on it, the hook had given way – because there were gold bars in the bag. 'I know specialised medicine's expensive,' I said, 'but I hope you're still taking plastic as well.'

I still get the mysterious deep ache. As one sinks deeper into the seventies, and the body wears down, things also happen to the inner self. The membrane shielding it from the world wears thin, and reality breaks in. Small worries metastasise into major problems. Your body's slower but your anger's quicker, and so, embarrassingly, are your tears. Hoarded frustrations and resentments emerge into the light, foibles ice into vices, setting you, as the saying goes, in your ways. You hang on to routine like a life preserver: the morning paper, the coffee break (from what?), the trip to the village, the slippers. There's a feeling of a penumbra descending, the gentlest of twilights, even of a morning.

And yet, and yet. The less flesh, the more spirit. Marriage's physicality maturing into companionship, the vicarious pleasures of grandparenting, walks in Carmel's idyllic garden, friendships cellared like fine wine, indifference to the opinions of the world. As the body threadbares, intimations of a folded inner self, packed as if for a journey – a journey that, even for the Christian, is mysterious, even terrifying.

A room of one's own in Wentworth Falls . . .

with garden outlook.

Going home

The great American novelist Saul Bellow wrote that we have no home city, but what comes increasingly to seem like one is the place where you grow up. The further I move from 4 Montague Avenue, the closer it gets, and before starting this memoir I flew down to Melbourne and made a pilgrimage there. It was an afternoon in April, the city's kindest month. Montague Avenue, set between a resonant network of Crimean War streets – Alma, Balaclava, Inkerman – was deserted. Poised in an autumnal haze, it offered up a peculiarly Melbourne middle classness. Trimmed lawns, hydrangeas, broad Californian bungalow verandahs – decorums, privacies: a hushed suburban stasis, as if I were dreaming the place.

When I reached the gatepost of number four – I can't go in, strangers have taken possession – I remembered the scorch marks it carried for years from the 1943 Guy Fawkes Night, when Mrs Kirkpatrick, our neighbour, ran out through the smoke and told us to go somewhere else. And as for you, she shouted, turning to Alan, older and bigger than the rest of us, that should be the fireworks up in New Guinea.

When we moved there in the late 1930s, Montague Avenue was raw and treeless, frontier territory, where gang wars were fought. One summer night, the big kids from the top of the street attacked those down below – the Wenden Grove gang. Too small to throw them far enough, I dug up stones for the Wenden Grove kids. As the artillery hurtled up and down my mother came to the gatepost and screamed for me to come home at once. As I retreated to our drive Murray M— was being carried down the adjoining one, with a great gash in his forehead. Four years later the Japanese would behead him in Rabaul.

There were many things I knew about this street that the street itself no longer knew – the fights, the football, the steaming manure left by the horses that drew the carts of the baker, the Chinese greengrocer, the milkman; the sonorities of David's cello from the house opposite as he went up and down the scales, the backyard air-raid shelters now filled in and forgotten, big Alan's footfalls as he did his nightly run round the block, the white feather he'd once found on his doormat, the hundreds of unwilling bike rides to school – once so dreaded that I got off round the corner, scratched my knee with a stone until it bled and came back home again, pretending I'd fallen off and hurt myself.

We were staying with our son Justin and his partner Kathryn at the time of this Melbourne visit, and after listening patiently as I reminisced after returning from Montague Avenue, he held up some printouts and said, 'There's more.' My cousin, who was the family genealogist, after months of my pleading had finally relented, and emailed his startling discoveries.

The family tradition that my paternal grandmother was an orphan was a fiction. Margaret Winifred Owen, the documents showed, was the daughter of one Barbara Mooney, a prostitute, who worked in Romeo Lane, off Bourke Street, opposite what was then the Eastern Markets.

According to her rap sheet, Barbara Mooney solicited so often she was jailed eleven times between 1867 and 1875, with extra days sometimes added in for insolence. Another document testified that at the age of five, Margaret Winifred 'was left in a Romeo Lane brothel, her head a mass of sores'. She was placed into guardianship in Abbotsford Convent, and licensed to Margaret Burns in 1896 to be apprenticed as a dressmaker.

Maybe Margaret Burns, who became a wonderful family

friend, and as an old lady in black took my brother and me everywhere, never told my father her secret – that his mother was not in fact an orphan but a neglected child. Whatever he knew, the half or full truth, he treated Burnie, as we called her, generously for the rest of her long life.

She outlived the fourteen-year-old she'd taken from the convent, who died in 1935 of pneumonia. My grandmother had re-invented herself. On her marriage certificate – to Albert Edward Oakley, my dour grandfather – she put her age down from thirty-four to twenty-nine, and her place of birth was changed from Pentridge Prison to South Yarra.

I have only two images of my grandmother. As a four-year-old I was taken to see her on her deathbed – the faintest of memories of a pale head topped by matted grey curls. The other is much clearer – it accompanied my boyhood for years. A portrait photograph that hung in our dining room of an elegant woman in an Edwardian ball gown, framed in gilt. I am a lady, it proclaimed to the world. (A lady who lived in a large house in Toorak.)

Some rapid googling revealed that unsavoury Romeo Lane was now Crossley Lane. Justin drove us there immediately. On the corner, fronted by the ever-popular Pelligrini's Espresso Bar, was a bigger, older building with a warren of rooms at the back. Was this where the brothel had once been, where my grandmother was rescued? It was getting dark, when the prostitutes would have been coming out. We were standing where my great-grandmother Barbara Mooney might have once stood, and this is where my narrative begins.

If we do have a home city, this is mine . . . Yarra dreaming.

Wakefield Press is an independent publishing and distribution company based in Adelaide, South Australia. We love good stories and publish beautiful books. To see our full range of titles, please visit our website at www.wakefieldpress.com.au.